Concentrate

Bonus study and revision support available **free,** online

online resource centre
www.oup.com/lawrevision/

Take your learning further:

➤ Multiple-choice questions

➤ Revision technique advice

➤ An interactive glossary

➤ Outline exam answers

➤ Flashcards of key cases

... and much more

To G and Boo, with love.

New to this edition

- Updates to the law to 1st January 2014, including the offences of stalking and squatting and cases such as *Sadique* (2013) and *Dawes* (2013)
- Enhanced chapter annotation
- More challenging essay titles and tables to improve learning

34SH
Ⓡ

Criminal Law
Concentrate

4th edition

Rebecca Huxley-Binns

Professor of Legal Education,
Nottingham Law School
National Teaching Fellow

OXFORD
UNIVERSITY PRESS

OXFORD

UNIVERSITY PRESS

Great Clarendon Street, Oxford, OX2 6DP,
United Kingdom

Oxford University Press is a department of the University of Oxford.
It furthers the University's objective of excellence in research, scholarship,
and education by publishing worldwide. Oxford is a registered trade mark of
Oxford University Press in the UK and in certain other countries

First edition 2009
Second edition 2011
Third edition 2013

Impression: 2

Public sector information reproduced under Open Government Licence v1.0
(http://www.nationalarchives.gov.uk/doc/open-government-licence/open-government-licence.htm)

Crown Copyright material reproduced with the permission of the
Controller, HMSO (under the terms of the Click Use licence)

Published in the United States of America by Oxford University Press
198 Madison Avenue, New York, NY 10016, United States of America

British Library Cataloguing in Publication Data

Data available

Library of Congress Control Number: 2014933492

ISBN 978-0-19-870375-4

Printed in Great Britain by
Ashford Colour Press Ltd, Gosport, Hampshire

Contents

Table of cases

Table of cases

✳✳✳✳✳✳✳✳✳✳✳✳

Table of cases

✳✳✳✳✳✳✳✳✳✳

Table of statutes

Table of statutes

✳✳✳✳✳✳✳✳✳✳

Table of statutes

International legislation

#1
The basis of criminal liability

Key facts

- The study of the **criminal law** is the study of liability.

- It is not about whether a person can be **charged** with a crime, or what **sentence** he may face if convicted, but rather it deals with whether a person is innocent or guilty of an offence (ie whether or not he can be convicted).

- Think about the criminal law in terms of *what* has to be proved in order to convict a person of a crime, not about *how* it can be proved.

- Your depth of understanding of the criminal law will also be enhanced if you are able to identify how the law is reformed, by Parliament, the courts, and as a result of any European influence.

Chapter overview

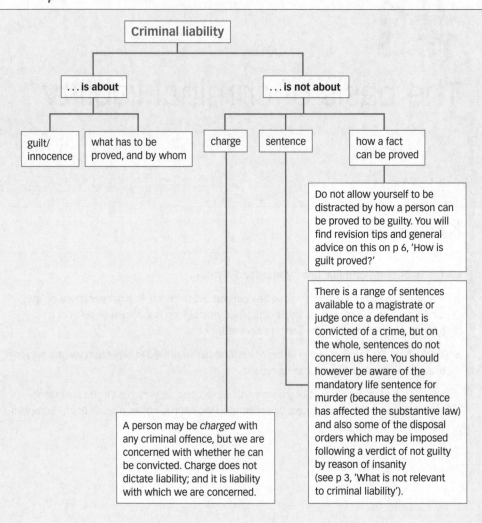

Criminal liability
What is criminal liability?

A person is criminally liable if he is guilty of an offence.

The criminal law consists of complex and sometimes contradictory rules which, when applied to a set of facts, allow us to conclude whether or not a person is guilty or not guilty of a crime. From the chapters which follow, you will see that we can reach a conclusion as to liability only by deciding whether the defendant (D) is responsible for the conduct that forms the basis of the charge (we call this the *actus reus*, see chapter 2), and he either had the prohibited state of mind (the *mens rea*, see chapter 3) or none was needed (for an offence of strict liability, see chapter 4) and there is no defence (see chapters 14 and 15). *What* has to be proved depends on the components (or elements) of the crime charged (chapters 5–13).

Revision tip

For each criminal offence on your syllabus (and that does not necessarily mean every offence covered in this book) you must know *each element*. You also need to know the source of the law (is it statutory or common law) and at least one (usually more) authority (case). Once you know these, you can build on that knowledge the more sophisticated arguments about whether the law is satisfactory, or how it should be reformed.

What is not relevant to criminal liability?

We are commonly not concerned with *why* D committed the crime. What we mean here is that D's motive is generally irrelevant to liability. If, for example, D stole goods from a shop to get the money to buy drugs to which he had an addiction, we consider only whether, on the facts, D committed theft. His addiction should not distract us from that question. However, the criminal law is not always blind to why a person commits a crime. For example, if D commits an assault because he is in danger from an aggressor, then the reason that D lashed out is certainly important as it may provide him with a defence (self-defence). Similarly, D may have killed his girlfriend because whilst experiencing an uncontrollable epileptic fit he hit her so hard she died. You may find it surprising, but such a defendant is probably insane (see further chapter 14).

Insanity is a curious defence, and the law has developed in such a way as to produce seemingly bizarre results; including labelling epilepsy as a form of insanity. The mention of insanity raises another point which must be made by way of introduction. Insanity is one of the only topics in the criminal law where the sentence may be relevant in your answer. For almost all other topics, you should not deal with sentencing at all. You may recall the very first sentence of this chapter—the criminal law is about liability. It is, therefore, not about punishment. (Sentencing and forms of punishment are usually taught as part of English Legal System and/or Criminology modules.) Insanity is different in this respect because an insane offender is not guilty by reason of that insanity, but he will be subject to a 'disposal' by the court. You should have a basic understanding of these disposal orders (see chapter 14) so you can show the examiner that you know the consequences of a successful plea of insanity. The only other sentence of which you must have some awareness is the mandatory sentence of imprisonment for murder; see chapter 7.

Most prosecutions are brought by the Crown Prosecution Service in the name of the Crown. It is very important that you understand that for the purposes of the criminal law, the question is not whether a person can be *charged* with an offence, but whether or not he can be convicted. As a matter of terminology, then, do not say, 'Alan can therefore be charged with theft', but after careful reasoning, using statutory provisions and cases in support, you may conclude, 'Alan is therefore guilty of the offence of theft'.

Burden of proof

What does burden of proof mean?

The **burden of proof** means the requirement on a party to adduce sufficient evidence to persuade the fact-finder (the magistrates or the jury), to a standard set by law, that a particular fact is true. For example, if a defendant is charged with murder, the burden of proving he is guilty lies on the prosecution who must do so beyond reasonable doubt.

Which party bears the burden of proof in criminal cases?

You are, no doubt, aware of the presumption of innocence, commonly phrased that a defendant is presumed to be innocent until proven guilty. This is a fundamental principle of the common law and is also one of the rights specifically mentioned to guarantee a fair trial according to **Article 6(2) European Convention on Human Rights**.

. . . .

Woolmington [1935] AC 462

The House of Lords held that there is a 'golden thread' running throughout the criminal law, that it is the duty of the prosecution to prove the defendant is guilty, not for the defendant to prove he is innocent. Viscount Sankey said the presumption of innocence is part of the common law 'and no attempt to whittle it down can be entertained'.

. . . .

In practice, this means that the defendant does not have to prove he is not guilty; the prosecution has to prove beyond reasonable doubt that he is. You should state the burden of proof is (almost always) on the prosecution. Even when dealing with *defences*, it is usually the prosecution's task to disprove the defence. This is because most defences are no more than a denial of an element of the crime, so the burden of proof remains on the prosecution. For example, the prosecution carries the burden of proof in relation to self-defence. So, if the defendant asserts that he was acting in self-defence, he does not have to prove he was; rather, the prosecution must prove he was not. That is not to say the defendant has no burden at all; he just does not have a burden of proof (also called a proof burden or a persuasive burden). He does, however, have a burden of raising the defence of self-defence. This is called being under an **evidential burden**. Evidential burdens are not proof burdens, but are duties to make issues 'live' in the case. You may sometimes see them referred to as burdens of 'passing the judge'. This means D must adduce enough evidence of the defence that the judge allows the defence to be put before the jury.

Revision Tip

In an exam, it is important to phrase your answers correctly. When discussing the criminal law, make sure you explain what the prosecution has to prove to obtain a conviction. If you find yourself writing that the defendant has to prove he is not guilty, or that he has to prove his defence (unless the next section of this book applies), cross out your answer and re-phrase it. For example:

- ~~Bert has the defence of self-defence on these facts. If he can prove his reaction was reasonable, he will be acquitted.~~
- Bert has the defence of self-defence on these facts. If he can adduce sufficient evidence for the judge to leave the defence to the jury, and if the prosecution cannot prove Bert was not acting in self-defence, Bert will be acquitted.

What is a reverse proof burden?

There are occasions on which the defendant has to prove a defence. In *Woolmington* [1935], Viscount Sankey explained the golden thread, and then added 'subject to what I have ... said about the defence of insanity and subject also to any statutory exception'.

There are certain defences which D must prove, and if he cannot, he may well be convicted. For almost all criminal law modules, the only defences where the defendant has to prove anything are:

- insanity, and

- diminished responsibility (s 2(2) **Homicide Act 1957** expressly states the defendant has to prove this defence).

Whenever the burden of proof is reversed to the defendant, he has to prove the defence on a balance of probabilities. We will return to proof issues where they arise throughout this book.

Do reverse proof burdens breach the presumption of innocence?

Article 6(2) ECHR provides that everyone charged with a criminal offence shall be presumed innocent until proved guilty according to law. All Acts of Parliament must be interpreted (as far as possible) to comply with this article (s 3 Human Rights Act 1998). Other than for insanity, reverse proof burdens are statutory, so a question that needs to be addressed is how judges should interpret any UK legislation which imposes a proof burden on D in light of Article 6(2). That is to say, can a defendant receive a fair trial under a statute (which must comply with Article 6) if the burden of proof of some element of the *defence* is reversed to him?

Burden of proof
✳✳✳✳✳✳✳✳✳✳

According to the House of Lords in *R v DPP, ex p Kebilene* [1999], the answer is a provisional 'yes', provided it is reasonable and proportionate to reverse that element to D, see *Salabiaku v France* (1998). Lord Steyn said in *R v Lambert* [2002] that the courts must focus on the extent to which the reversal is connected to the moral dimension of the offence through the *mens rea* requirement, which is closely linked to another key issue—whether the offence is 'truly criminal' or merely regulatory in nature. He continued that the burden is on the state to show that the legislative means were not greater than necessary. The leading case on the burden of proof, and reverse proof burdens, is the conjoined appeals of *Sheldrake v DPP; AG Ref (No 4 of 2002)* [2005] which you will find in 'Key cases' on p 9.

How is guilt proved?

There are extensive rules of evidence governing the admissibility of evidence which do not concern us here. One of the most common questions which taxes a student of the criminal law, though, is how the prosecution can prove what D was thinking. Certainly, if the crime has a *mens rea* requirement (see chapter 3), failure by the prosecution to prove the *mens rea* means D will be acquitted. However, you must resist the temptation to be distracted by this. Suffice to say (and once said, you must move on), *mens rea* can be proved because the fact-finder (usually the jury for our purposes) *infers* it from what D did or did not do. **Section 8 Criminal Justice Act 1967** provides:

A court or jury, in determining whether a person has committed an offence—

(a) shall not be bound in law to infer that he intended or foresaw a result of his actions by reasons only of its being a natural and probable consequence of those actions; but

(b) shall decide whether he did intend or foresee that result by reference to all the evidence, drawing such inferences from the evidence as appear proper in the circumstances.

Revision tip

You will find it useful to weave proof into your revision notes. You might wish to write postcards for each of the main offences and defences. You could phrase your notes in terms of what has to be proved:

Offence—murder (see chapter 7)
What has to be proved? The *prosecution* must prove that:
- D killed **the victim** (V) under the Queen's Peace (the *actus reus*), and
- D intended to kill or cause serious harm (the *mens rea*).

Defence—insanity (see chapter 14)
What has to be proved? The *defendant* must prove on a balance of probabilities that:
- he was suffering from a defect of reason
- arising from a disease of mind so that

- he did not know the nature and quality of his act, or
- he did not know it was wrong.

Reform of the criminal law

You may have heard the phrase that the law is an ass. There are, at least, some curiosities and there are many inconsistencies in the criminal law. One of the statute laws still in force is over 150 years old; so too are some of the case authorities. Consequently, some are in desperate need of reform.

Revision Tip

You must always have a critical eye when studying the criminal law. In essay questions in particular, some evaluative comments are required. Do not accept that, just because the law is 'x', that 'x' is therefore morally or ethically 'right'.

The Law Commission is very active in the field of the criminal law (see lawcommission. justice.gov.uk). In 1989, the Law Commission published a full Draft Criminal Code: *Criminal law: a criminal code for England and Wales* (Law Com No 177, 1989). It was a huge report and contained recommendations for the codification of the whole of the criminal law of England and Wales. On reflection, it was more than Parliament could cope with in terms of the volume of legislative change required, so the Law Commission took on smaller, discrete tasks. This piecemeal approach attracted more political support, and the Law Commission has since enjoyed considerable success, seeing many of its recommendations for reform reach the statute books.

Revision Tip

You are strongly advised to be aware of the main proposals for laws which have not yet been changed. There are two good reasons why. First, if you are able to see how the Law Commission thinks the law should be changed, you will be able to give an evaluative comment on the current state of the law, and this will get you marks. Secondly, the Law Commission's proposals might be in force by the time you get into practice (if that is your ultimate wish), so the earlier you familiarise yourself with the proposals, the better off you will be when advising your clients.

✔ *Looking for extra marks?*

Your examiner will give you credit if you can state and apply the current law correctly, but there will be more credit if you are then able to show the examiner how the outcome might differ under the key proposals for reform. You would also do very well to be able to give a brief indication of which outcome is to be preferred, and why.

Judicial reform of the criminal law

On the theme of change to the criminal law, judicial reform is unlikely to occur on a large scale. Judges cannot create new criminal offences, and can develop existing laws only within the rules of precedent (*stare decisis*) and then only where the facts of the case before them give rise to that legal issue (*Shaw v DPP* [1962]). You should therefore have an awareness of the judicial developments in the criminal law that occur during your studies, but for wholesale reform, watch carefully the proposals of the Law Commission and Parliament.

Influences of Europe

Another key reform in the criminal justice system is, of course, the **Human Rights Act 1998** which provides that English law must comply, if possible, with the Articles in the **European Convention on Human Rights 1950**. Most students are able to cite **Article 6**, at least, which is the right to a fair trial. It may, however, surprise you to learn that the Act has had very little impact on the substantive criminal law. One of the reasons is because **Article 6** is limited to procedural matters (the rules on the admissibility of evidence, etc) and not the substantive criminal law (the rules which govern liability). The Act is not totally without effect, however. Two articles in particular have the potential to impact the substantive criminal law. **Article 2** provides for the right to life, and this has an effect where a person uses self-defence to kill an aggressor (see 'Self-defence and the right to life' in chapter 15, p 193). **Article 7**, which in essence provides that the criminal law must be reasonably certain so people can predict whether their conduct may contravene the criminal law, might yet have an impact on a few key crimes; notably strict liability offences (see 'Can strict liability be justified?' in chapter 4, p 47), manslaughter by gross negligence ('Gross negligence manslaughter' in chapter 8, p 103) and the element of dishonesty in theft ('Dishonesty' in chapter 11, p 144).

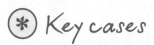 **Key cases**

Case	Facts	Principle
Lambert [2002] 2 AC 545	D appealed against his conviction for possession of a class A drug with intent to supply. He had been found in possession of a bag containing a drug but said he neither knew, nor suspected, nor had reason to suspect the nature of the contents of the bag. The question on appeal was whether he had to prove his lack of knowledge of the contents, or if the prosecution had to prove he did know. The section in issue was **s 28 Misuse of Drugs Act 1971**.	**Section 28**, insofar as it contained an express reverse proof burden, should be 'read down' as imposing an evidential burden only on the accused (note: this is in fact **obiter** as the majority of the House held that the **Human Rights Act 1998** did not have retrospective application).

Case	Facts	Principle
Sheldrake v DPP; AG Ref (No 4 of 2002) [2005] 1 AC 264	*Sheldrake* D was convicted of drink-driving. He appealed on the ground that the defence, which cast upon the defendant the burden of proving that there was no likelihood of his driving the vehicle while over the limit, violated his right to a fair trial under **Article 6**.	The House of Lords held that the allocation of a proof burden to the accused did not violate Article 6. It was directed to a legitimate objective (the prevention of death, injury, and damage caused by unfit drivers); and the likelihood of the defendant driving was a matter so closely conditioned by his own knowledge as to make it much more appropriate for him to prove on a balance of probabilities that he would not have been likely to drive than for the prosecution to prove, beyond reasonable doubt, that he would. In addition, the imposition of a legal burden on D did not go beyond what was necessary and reasonable, and was not in any way arbitrary.
	AG Ref D was charged with two offences relating to terrorism (belonging to and professing to belong to a proscribed organisation). The appeal concerned the elements of the offences and related defences, and who had to prove them.	The House held that if there was a reverse proof burden, there was a real risk that a person who was innocent of any blameworthy or properly criminal conduct, but who was unable to establish a defence to one of these charges, might nevertheless be convicted. The provisions in question therefore breached the presumption of innocence.
Woolmington [1935] AC 462	D was charged with murder. The trial judge directed the jury that, once the prosecution had proved a person had died at D's hands, it was for D to prove it was not murder.	Viscount Sankey held that the burden of proof lies on the prosecution, and that includes proof of each element of the crime, and the elements of any defence, other than the defence of insanity and other 'statutory provisions'.

Key debates

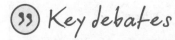 Key debates

Topic	Reform of the law; who does it and how they do it
Author/Academic	Professor Sir John Smith QC
Viewpoint	Examines and evaluates the roles of academics, judges, and Parliament in reforming the criminal law.
Source	'Judge, jurist and Parliament', Judicial Studies Board Annual Lecture 2002, available at www.smithy.org/JSB_Judge_Jurist_Parliament.pdf

#2
Actus reus

Key facts

- The **elements of an offence** are found in the definition of the offence, and that is contained in a statute or in cases (common law).

- These elements are known as the **definitional elements** of the offence.

- The definitional elements are broken down, to manage them more easily, into ***actus reus*** and *mens rea*.

- The *actus reus* consists of prohibited conduct (acts or omissions), prohibited circumstances, and/or prohibited consequences (results).

- A person can be criminally liable for failing to act (ie an omission), but imposing criminal liability for an omission can be controversial.

- **Causation** is a key part of consequence/result crimes. The prosecution must prove that the result was caused by the defendant. In order to do this, the **chain of causation** must first be established, and then consideration must be given to any intervention which might break the chain.

Chapter overview

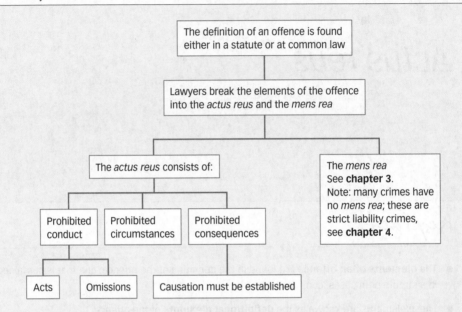

The definition of an offence is found either in a statute or at common law

Lawyers break the elements of the offence into the *actus reus* and the *mens rea*

The *actus reus* consists of:

Prohibited conduct

Prohibited circumstances

Prohibited consequences

The *mens rea*
See **chapter 3**.
Note: many crimes have no *mens rea*; these are strict liability crimes, see **chapter 4**.

Acts

Omissions

Causation must be established

What is *actus reus*?

Identifying the definitional elements of an offence

We saw in chapter 1 that criminal liability is found when the prosecution can prove the defendant satisfies the elements of the crime, and has no defence. The elements of each offence (and of each defence) are found in its definition, and the definition is found either at common law (cases only) or under statute (an Act of Parliament, supplemented by case law which interprets the statutory provision).

Note: In this chapter and the next two, we are concerned with *offences* only and not defences.

The first step is to take the definition of a crime and see if you can break it down into its components. We are going quickly to look at two offences which are commonly taught on a criminal law module. Even if you are already familiar with the two crimes, it is still worth reading what follows to see how the elements have been identified.

Revision tip

For each offence on your syllabus, make sure you are able to recite *each* element. If there are five elements to a crime, you must know all five; you cannot explain and apply only four of them and still reach a sensible conclusion as to liability!

How to identify the definitional elements of gross negligence manslaughter

Our first crime is the *common law* offence of manslaughter by gross negligence. In the leading case, *Adomako* [1994], Lord Mackay, the then Lord Chancellor, delivered the leading speech of a unanimous House of Lords. He said 'the ordinary principles of the law of negligence apply to ascertain whether or not the defendant has been in breach of a duty of care towards the victim who has died. If such breach of duty is established the next question is whether that breach of duty caused the death of the victim. If so, the jury must go on to consider whether that breach of duty should be characterised as gross negligence and therefore as a crime.'

We can therefore conclude that the elements of the offence are:

- a duty of care exists between D and V
- which is breached
- (we shall see in chapter 8 that the breach of duty must involve a risk of death)
- which caused V to die
- *and* the jury finds the breach serious enough to be a crime.

What is *actus reus*?

✱✱✱✱✱✱✱✱✱✱

> ### ✅ Looking for extra marks?
>
> Did you notice in the explanation of the case (*Adomako*) above, we named the judge who delivered the speech, and we pointed out that the decision was at the House of Lords, and that it was unanimous? *Do not revise this detail at the expense of knowing the decision in the case*, but if you are able to remember this type of detail (for the leading cases), you can use the information in the exam to point out the importance of the case (for example: there were no dissents).

How to identify the definitional elements of criminal damage

An example of a *statutory* offence is criminal damage. This is governed by s 1 Criminal Damage Act 1971, which provides:

> A person who without lawful excuse destroys or damages any property belonging to another intending to destroy or damage any such property or being reckless as to whether any such property would be destroyed or damaged shall be guilty of an offence.

The definitional elements of the crime could therefore be listed as:

- without lawful excuse
- D destroys or damages
- any property
- belonging to another
- intending to or being reckless as to whether any such property would be destroyed or damaged.

> ### Revision tip
>
> What we have done for each of the examples above is break the offence into its constituent elements; and once you can do this with confidence for any offence you come across, you will never forget how to do it.
>
> Once you can list the elements, the next step in your revision is to add cases for each element, including the key facts and *ratio decidendi*, and then add some commentary on the case, particularly if it has been criticised.

To make offences easier to handle, lawyers split the crime into two parts which we call the *actus reus* and the *mens rea*.

What does *actus reus* mean?

Have another look at the offence of criminal damage above. It has been broken into five elements. Criminal damage consists of conduct (destroying or damaging), in particular circumstances (property belonging to another) with a particular state of mind (intending or being reckless to the elements above). Most criminal offences have similar constituent elements. We classify the elements as either *actus reus* or *mens rea*, from the Latin phrase *actus non facit reum nisi mens sit rea*. The phrase translates into English as 'the act is not guilty unless the mind is guilty'. Hence the *actus* (act) must be *reum* (guilty) and the *mens* (mind) must also be *rea* (guilty). We examine *mens rea* in chapter 3. We tackle *actus reus* here.

The definition of actus reus

The strict translation of *actus reus* to 'guilty act' is misleading. *Actus reus* does not *necessarily* denote 'guilt' in terms of blameworthiness or moral wrongness, but refers to the prohibited conduct, circumstance, or result (or a combination of them). Secondly, the *actus reus* does not have to be an act; the conduct could be satisfied by an omission (see p 16, 'Omissions'). Thirdly, *actus reus* includes far more than conduct. The term is used to cover any circumstances mentioned in the definition of the offence and any consequence (or result) too.

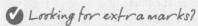 **Looking for extra marks?**

If you are answering an essay question on *actus reus* in the exam, you might find it useful to know that the Law Commission (among others) has called for the term *actus reus* to be replaced with 'external elements' and *mens rea* with 'fault elements' to reflect better their true meanings. Lord Diplock in *Miller* [1983] said that it would be 'conducive to clarity ... if we were to avoid bad Latin and instead to think and speak ... about the conduct of the accused and his state of mind at the time of that conduct, instead of speaking of *actus reus* and *mens rea*'.

By far the easiest way to find the *actus reus* is to take away the *mens rea* (chapter 3) and what is left must be *actus reus*, even if that consists of the state of mind of V (eg V's consent, or rather the lack of it, in the offence of rape). So, returning to criminal damage for a moment, the *actus reus* of criminal damage is therefore:

- destroying or damaging
- any property
- belonging to another.

The element 'without lawful excuse' is probably another element of the *actus reus*, but might be a defence. Do not worry about this lack of certainty. Judges have struggled for decades to decide whether what we call defences are in fact defences (ie they exist separately from the *actus reus* and *mens rea*) or are part of the *actus reus* or *mens rea*. It is not your job to make this decision for them. It is your job, ultimately, to decide (i) if it matters, and (ii) if it does, what the consequences are, and (iii) which is preferable. You will be relieved to know that this issue does not have to concern us again until chapter 14.

Conduct

Acts and omissions

Some crimes can be committed either by doing something (ie a positive act) or by not doing something (ie an omission). An example of a crime that can be committed by either act or omission is murder. If D intentionally stabs V and V dies, that is murder by an act. On the other hand, if D is under a legal responsibility to care for V, and D deliberately fails to feed V, and V dies, that is murder by omission (see *Gibbins and Proctor* (1918) in 'Familial relationships' on p 17).

Some crimes, however, can only be committed by an act because that is what the definition of the crime says. For example, the offence of robbery (see 'Robbery' in chapter 13, p 16) could not be committed without D actually doing something (such as using force, or threatening to use force, etc in order to steal). On the other hand, some crimes can be committed only by omission. For example, s 36 Road Traffic Act 1988 provides that a person who drives a vehicle and who fails to comply with a road sign (such as a 'stop' sign) is guilty of an offence. It is the failure to comply which gives rise to criminal liability.

Voluntariness

Whether the *actus reus* is committed by an act or by omission, it must be committed voluntarily. Conduct which is involuntary in law is conduct which is not subject to D's conscious will. This may be because of an uncontrollable impulse, such as to close one's eyes when one sneezes, or it may be as a result of an unanticipated and serious side-effect of taking prescription medication. Where D's conduct amounts to the *actus reus* of a crime, but is involuntary, we *say* he has the defence of **automatism**, but it is *actually* a denial of *actus reus*.

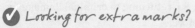 **Looking for extra marks?**

Refer to the chapters on the defences (chapters 14 and 15), and make sure you are able to state which are 'true' defences and those which are assertions which amount to a denial of one or more of the definitional elements of the crime.

We return to the 'defence' of **automatism** in chapter 14.

Omissions

The common law traditionally prohibits acts and does not criminalise omissions. Therefore no liability will usually arise in relation to a failure to act. There are some good reasons for this approach, including:

- imposing liability for an offence of failing to act would be hard if not impossible to enforce,

- proving causation might be impossible,
- conflicting with the principle of autonomy; that is, we choose how and when to act and we are individually responsible for our conduct, but should not be responsible for the conduct of others. Imposing criminal liability for failing to assist others conflicts with this principle.

Revision Tip
Essay questions often ask you to evaluate the circumstances in which the law will and will not impose liability for an omission. You should have read this topic in at least one of the standard textbooks thoroughly.

However, the law does prohibit certain omissions (as the exception rather than the rule) where two conditions are satisfied:

1. the offence in question is capable of being committed by omission (examples are given above), and
2. D is under a legal duty to act, either at common law or under statute.

Liability for omissions at common law

The common law recognises that duties arise in only some circumstances or categories. You will find an illustration of the categories of duty, and leading cases, with some commentary in the case boxes, but you should supplement this with wider and deeper reading from the standard textbooks.

Duties may arise in situations of

Contract

Pittwood (1902) 19 TLR 37

D worked as a level-crossing operator. He forgot to close the gate and V was killed by a train. D's contractual duties were used to find a duty because his breach of contract endangered the public.

Familial relationships

Gibbins and Proctor (1918) 13 Cr App R 134

D (V's father) and D2 (V's stepmother) deliberately failed to feed V, who died. D and D2 were both convicted of murder. D owed V a duty as parent, but D2 also owed a duty as she had assumed *de facto* (meaning in reality or as good as) parental responsibility.

Omissions

✴✴✴✴✴✴✴✴✴✴

Assumption of responsibility

....

Airedale NHS Trust v Bland [1993] AC 789

This civil case deals with complex issues about the duty of care owed by doctors to patients. Among other things, the case permits a doctor to stop caring for or treating a patient, where it is in the patient's best interests. What is not decided in law is whether the duty arises simply by way of contract, a result of assumption of responsibility, or by the doctor's oath (the Hippocratic oath), or a combination.

....

Stone and Dobinson [1977] 2 All ER 341

D (V's sister) and D2 (D's partner) were convicted of manslaughter. D and D2 had failed to summon help for V, who had died whilst under their care. V had been anorexic and had refused to eat. The Court of Appeal held there was a legal duty, not just because V was D's sister, but also because V lived in D's and D2's house, and they had voluntarily assumed a duty to act by their attempts to care for her. The decision is controversial and you are strongly advised to read commentary on it.

....

Khan and Khan [1998] Crim LR 830

The Court of Appeal allowed Ds' appeals against convictions for manslaughter. They were drug dealers and had not summoned assistance for V, a drug user, when she had fallen into a coma. The Court of Appeal said that to impose a duty in such circumstances would add to the categories of recognised duties of care. However, compare with:

....

Ruffell [2003] 2 Cr App R (S) 53

D and V had each self-injected with drugs. When V showed signs of overdose, D first tried to revive him and then left V outside his house. D telephoned V's mother asking her to collect her son. V later died of hypothermia and opiate intoxication. D owed V a duty of care; he had assumed the duty when he tried to revive him, and breached it when he left him outside in the cold.

....

Evans [2009] 1 WLR 1999

D gave her sister heroin. The sister self-administered it. The Court of Appeal held that a duty arose when D realised her sister had overdosed and did not summon medical help. Lord Judge CJ held:

> when a person has created or contributed to the creation of a state of affairs which he knows, or ought reasonably to know, has become life threatening, a consequent duty on him to act by taking reasonable steps to save the other's life will normally arise.

....

Danger, where D is responsible for creating the danger

Miller [1983] 1 All ER 978

D, a squatter, fell asleep smoking a cigarette. When he woke up, he realised a fire had started, but did not extinguish it or summon help. The House of Lords held that even where the original conduct was inadvertent, when D subsequently became aware of the danger he had caused, he was under a duty to prevent or reduce the risk by his own efforts, or if necessary by summoning the fire brigade.

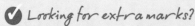 **Looking for extra marks?**

The principle in *Miller* has clearly been extended in *Ruffell* and *Evans* (p 18). Consider how far the *Miller* principle might be taken.

DPP v Santana-Bermudez [2004] Crim LR 471

This case extended the *Miller* principle to include the situation where the original conduct was advertent and there was a reasonably foreseeable risk of injury to another. D failed to inform a uniformed officer searching D's pockets that there were exposed hypodermic syringes in those pockets.

Public office

Dytham (1979) 69 Cr App R 387

A uniformed police officer stood and watched a man being beaten and kicked to death in the gutter from only 30 yards away. The officer made no move to intervene or summon assistance. He was convicted of the common law offence of misconduct of an officer.

Liability for failing to act under statute

Statutory liability for an omission is not unusual and there are hundreds of crimes which either are capable of being committed by omission, or can be committed only by omission. When we looked at the offence of criminal damage in 'How to identify the definitional elements of criminal damage' on p 14, we noticed the result required is destroying or damaging. As you can see from *Miller*, it is possible to commit this offence by inaction (provided there is a duty). Criminal damage may therefore be committed by an act or an omission. For an offence which may be committed only by omission, consider s 84 Companies Act 2006:

Circumstances

[W]here a company fails, without reasonable excuse, to comply with any specified requirement of regulations ... an offence is committed by—

1. the company, and
2. every officer of the company who is in default ...

Circumstances

The circumstances mentioned in the definition of the crime are also part of the *actus reus* of the offence. The age of the complainant in **s 7 Sexual Offences Act 2007** is one example (subsec (1)(c)):

(1) A person commits an offence if—

    (a) he intentionally touches another person,

    (b) the touching is sexual, and

    (c) the other person is under 13.

In the offence of criminal damage examined on p 14, the circumstances of the offence are that the property belongs to another.

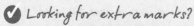 Looking for extra marks?

Larsonneur (1934) is often considered to illustrate a crime without *actus reus*, but the crime committed *does* have an *actus reus*; the circumstances. Read the case, or at least a summary of it, and explain the *actus reus* of the crime.

Causation

Causation is only an issue for result crimes; that is, crimes which have a result or consequence specified in the offence definition. Examples of result crimes include:

- murder (ie death), and
- causing grievous bodily harm with intent (ie grievous bodily harm).

For any result crime, the prosecution must prove the defendant *caused* the result.

A preliminary point must be made: You must not ask *what* caused the result? But, *did D cause the result?*

This is very important. Why?

1. There could be a number of competing, conflicting, or contributory causes and, as we shall see, your task is not to sort out which is the sole or even the main cause, but

2. because it is the liability *of the defendant* that has to be considered where causation is an issue, his liability depends on proof that *he* caused the result. If he did not, he is not liable for that crime.

To establish a chain of causation, first D's act must *in law* have caused the result. Secondly, that factual chain must also exist *in law*, and thirdly, it must not be broken by an intervention.

It is unusual for causation to be in issue as a matter of fact, or of law, or both, but if it is necessary to establish that D did cause the result, the opening part of the chart in Figure 2.1 applies. Even if a chain of causation is established (ie D can be said to have made a sufficient contribution in fact and in law to the outcome) it does not automatically mean D caused the result, because a new act might break the chain.

Figure 2.1 Establishing the chain of causation

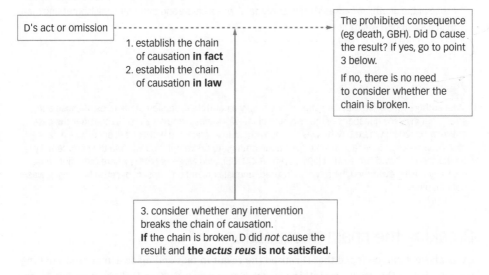

Establishing the chain of causation in fact

If the result would have happened anyway, then causation has not occurred in fact. The question which must be asked is this: *but for* D's conduct, would the result have happened? If the answer is 'no', D *has* factually caused the result. If the answer is 'yes', D *has not* caused the result.

. . . .

White [1910] 2 KB 124

D had put cyanide in his mother's drink, but she died of unrelated heart failure and no cyanide was found in her body. D had not caused her death, so he could not be convicted of murder.

. . . .

Establishing the chain of causation in law

The next step, once factual causation is established, is to ensure D is also the cause in law. The law is clear that if D's conduct was *a* cause, and that does not mean the only or even the main cause, he can be found to have been the legal cause of the result.

....

Kimsey [1996] Crim LR 35

D was charged with causing death by dangerous driving. He and V had been racing each other in their cars at very high speed. Their cars collided and V's car spun out of control and was hit by an oncoming car. The Court of Appeal upheld the judge's direction that the jury could find D had caused V's death even if they were not sure that D's driving 'was the principal, or a substantial, cause of the death, as long as you are sure that it was a cause and that there was something more than a slight or a trifling link'.

....

✔️ *Looking for extra marks?*

Most authors recognise that causation is not simply a neutral application of the rules of cause and effect, but involves questions of morality and blameworthiness. You may wish to consider the case of *Williams* [2011] where D (who was driving without insurance and without a licence) was *a* cause of V's death despite the fact D could have done nothing to prevent it. You will find the commentary on the case by David Ormerod at [2011] Crim LR 474. See also *Hughes* [2013] where D did not cause death by driving even though he was uninsured, unqualified and unlicensed, because his *driving* was not at fault.

Breaking the chain of causation

Even where it can be found that D caused the result in fact *and* made a 'more than trifling' contribution to the result, something might have occurred after D's act or omission, and before the result, which breaks the link (the so-called chain of causation) between D and the consequence. If that is the case, D is not liable for the offence. Indeed, even though D did make a 'more than trifling contribution', legal causation is ultimately not satisfied if the chain of causation is subsequently broken.

An intervention is called a *novus actus interveniens*, or new intervening act. Whether a *novus actus interveniens* does break the chain of causation depends on what type of intervention it is, and what legal test is adopted.

Natural events

If the natural event was not reasonably foreseeable, it breaks the chain of causation. There is no case law here, but most standard textbooks illustrate this by example (eg the incoming tide).

Victim's acts

If the victim's act was not reasonably foreseeable, it breaks the chain of causation.

Williams [1992] 2 All ER 183

V jumped from the moving car being driven by D. It is possible D threatened to rob V, but on appeal it was held that V's reaction was unforeseeable. In **Roberts (1971)** V jumped from a moving car because D, the driver, had made unwanted sexual advances. V's reaction was reasonably foreseeable and did not break the chain of causation.

Blaue [1975] 1 WLR 1411

The victim of wounding declined, on religious grounds, a blood transfusion which would have saved her life. This did not break the causal connection between the act of wounding and death. D was not entitled to claim that the victim's refusal of medical treatment because of her religious beliefs was unreasonable.

Revision tip

Can you explain why Vs' reactions in the aforementioned cases above were (un)reasonable? It is important you are able to apply the law to similar factual circumstances in problem questions in the exam.

However, if the victim's act was free and voluntary, it does break the chain of causation.

Kennedy [2008] 1 AC 269

At the victim's request, D prepared a syringe of heroin and gave it to V. V self-injected. V died. The House of Lords allowed D's appeal, holding that where a defendant has been involved in the supply of a class A drug, which is then freely and voluntarily self-administered by the person to whom it was supplied, and the administration of the drug then causes his death, D has not caused the death where V is a fully informed and responsible adult.

Third party acts

The free, deliberate, and informed act of a third party breaks the chain of causation.

Paggett (1983) 76 Cr App R 279

There was a shoot-out between D and the police. D held V in front of him as a human shield. In returning fire, the police shot and killed V. The Court of Appeal said that occasionally the intervention of a third person might break the causal chain, but a reasonable act performed in self-defence does not.

....

....

Jordan (1956) 40 Cr App R 152

V was given a large volume of medicine to which he had previously shown intolerance. This was described as abnormal medical treatment and it broke the chain of causation between D (who had stabbed V) and V's death. The chain was not broken however in *Smith* [1959]. Although V's death only occurred after he had suffered a series of unfortunate events (including being dropped and being given the wrong medical treatment), the stabbing by D was an 'operating and substantial cause' of V's death. Similarly, in *Cheshire* [1991], V did not die until two months after being shot by D. The Court of Appeal held that even though medical negligence was the immediate cause of V's death, it did not exclude D's responsibility. The negligence was not so independent of D's acts, and in itself so potent in causing death, that D's acts could be regarded as insignificant.

....

The legal principle from the case of *Malcherek* [1981] is that a doctor who switches off a life-support machine is not the cause of the death where V was originally and criminally injured by D.

....

Environment Agency v Empress Car Co [1999] 2 AC 22

In a decision which appears inconsistent with those above, the defendant company stored diesel in a tank which had an unlocked tap on it. The tap was opened by a person unknown and the entire contents ran down the drain into the river. The charge was *causing* pollution; the issue was whether the act of the unknown person broke the chain of causation. The House of Lords held the principle was not whether the third party's act was free, deliberate, and informed but whether it was something normal (which it was) or something extraordinary (which it was not).

This decision was approved in *Kennedy* [2008] (HL), but limited to the specific statute in question.

....

 **Key cases**

Details of the key cases on liability for *omissions* are found in the case boxes earlier in this chapter.

Airedale NHS Trust v Bland [1993] AC 789
DPP v Santana-Bermudez [2004] Crim LR 471

Dytham (1979) 69 Cr App R 387
Evans [2009] 1 WLR 1999
Gibbins and Proctor (1918) 13 Cr App R 134
Khan and Khan [1998] Crim LR 830
Miller [1983] 1 All ER 978
Pittwood (1902) 19 TLR 37
Ruffell [2003] 2 Cr App R (S) 53
Stone and Dobinson [1977] 2 All ER 341

Details of the key cases on **causation** are found in the case boxes earlier in this chapter.

Blaue [1975] 1 WLR 1411
Cheshire [1991] 1 WLR 844
Environment Agency v Empress Car Co [1999] 2 AC 22
Jordan (1956) 40 Cr App R 152
Kennedy [2008] 1 AC 269
Kimsey [1996] Crim LR 35
Malcherek [1981] 1 WLR 690
Paggett (1983) 76 Cr App R 279
Roberts (1971) 56 Cr App R 95
Smith [1959] 2 QB 35
Williams [1992] 2 All ER 183

Key debates

Topic	'Liability for omissions in criminal law'
Author/Academic	JC Smith
Viewpoint	Reviews omissions liability; discusses whether it is the rule or the exception; analyses whether the distinction is helpful; examines how the wording of an offence can influence the finding of liability; considers the overlap between omissions and the continuing transaction theory (*Fagan* [1968]).
Source	(1984) 4 Legal Studies 88

Topic	'Criminal omissions—the conventional view'
Author/Academic	Glanville Williams
Viewpoint	Critically analyses the reasons for duties arising; analyses the moral duty to act and the legal duty; and if there is a difference; and if there is, whether there is a justification.
Source	(1991) 107 LQR 86

Topic	The law governing causation
Author/Academic	HLA Hart and T Honoré
Viewpoint	Widely regarded as the authoritative textbook on causation in the criminal law.
Source	*Causation in the Law*, OUP, 2nd edn, 1985

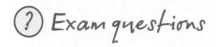

Exam questions

Problem question

During a criminal law tutorial, an argument erupted between two students, Andrew and Mark, about the defence of insanity. Andrew picked up one of his biggest textbooks and threw it at Mark with intent to cause serious harm. Mark ducked, and the book's spine struck Kirin, another student, on her temple. Kirin fell unconscious.

Jane, the law lecturer, directed two other students, Sandeep and Samantha, to carry Kirin to the reception area where Jane could telephone for an ambulance. Unfortunately, Sandeep and Samantha banged Kirin's head against the door frame as they left, exacerbating Kirin's injuries.

When the ambulance arrived, Kirin was taken immediately to the hospital. She had a brain scan. A junior doctor misread the scan and wrongly decided Kirin needed urgent brain surgery.

Kirin lapsed into a coma during the operation and doctors subsequently indicated there was no chance of recovery. With Kirin's family's agreement, they turned off the machines keeping Kirin alive. Kirin died.

Andrew is charged with the murder of Kirin. Discuss his criminal liability, if any.

An outline answer is included at the end of the book.

Essay question

Culpable inaction is always less blameworthy than culpable action.

Critically consider when criminal liability may arise in respect of an omission.

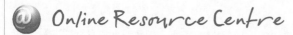

@ Online Resource Centre

To see an outline answer to this question log on to www.oxfordtextbooks.co.uk/orc/concentrate/

#3
Mens rea

- ***Mens rea*** means guilty mind, but the term is better thought of as the fault element of the offence.

- The role of *mens rea* is to attribute fault or blameworthiness (also called culpability) to the *actus reus*.

- The main types of *mens rea* are intention, recklessness, and negligence.

- The judiciary has encountered difficulties in defining, in particular, intention and recklessness.

- Issues may arise when the *mens rea* and *actus reus* do not coincide in time.

- The doctrine of **transferred malice** allows *mens rea* to be transferred from the intended victim to the unintended victim, in certain situations.

Chapter overview

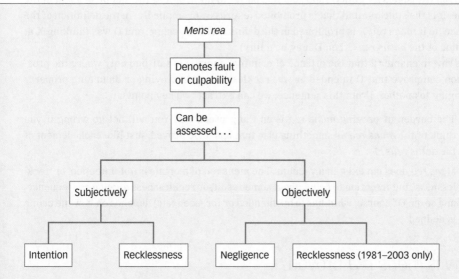

Introduction

Mens rea translates as 'guilty mind', but it is better to think of it as the mental element of the crime. It is the state of mind that is prohibited (expressly or impliedly) in the definition of the offence (ie if *mens rea* X is prohibited in the definition of the crime, and D was thinking X at the time of the *actus reus*, then D may be guilty).

We saw in chapter 2 that the offence of criminal damage is satisfied only where the prosecution can prove that D intended or was reckless about destroying or damaging property belonging to another. From this sentence, we can extract two key points:

- The burden of proving *mens rea* is on the prosecution. You will not go wrong if you think of the *mens rea* as something else that has to be proved, just like each element of the *actus reus*.

- *Mens rea* does not exist in a vacuum. The *mens rea* of a crime is *not* 'intention' or 'recklessness', but intention to *bring about* some result, or recklessness *about* a consequence, and so on. Of course, *what* has to be intended or foreseen (etc) depends on how the crime is defined.

How is *mens rea* proved?

A study of *mens rea* is a study of *what* needs to be proved, and as we already pointed out in chapter 1, criminal liability is not about *how* it can be proved. That said, students can easily become distracted by the question of how the prosecution can prove what D was thinking. The jury can *infer* what D was thinking from the evidence (see **s 8 Criminal Justice Act 1967** under 'How is guilt proved?' in chapter 1, p 6).

Take a very straightforward example; at D's trial for murder, the prosecution adduces evidence of emails and text messages that D sent to V, expressing D's hatred of V and threatening to kill V. V was later found, stabbed to death. D was standing over V's body, laughing and holding the knife which was later established to be the murder weapon. The prosecution can prove that at the time of the death D intended to kill V or cause GBH if the jury infers that D intended to kill or cause GBH to V.

We accept this is a pretty obvious example, and there are more factually ambiguous examples that may be given but it distracts us to consider it further. To emphasise: we are concerned with *what* has to be proved, not *how*.

Fault

As we saw in chapter 2, there are those who have called for the abolition of the terms *actus reus* and *mens rea*. One of the reasons is that the direct translation of *mens rea* to 'guilty mind' is misleading. For example, gross negligence manslaughter, which is a crime with a *mens rea* of gross negligence, is often wrongly described by students as having no *mens rea* at all.

The Law Commission prefers the term 'fault element' to *mens rea*, and there are certainly good reasons for changing our lexicon. First, it would prevent students suggesting that crimes with objective *mens rea*s are crimes of strict liability; and secondly, it would focus our mind on the role *mens rea* plays in criminal liability, which is to describe the fault or blameworthiness of the crime. Performing the *actus reus* deliberately is seen as being worse than performing it foreseeing the risk of the prohibited consequence, and deciding to take the risk; which is in turn viewed as worse than acting without thinking about the risk at all. There are therefore degrees of mental wrongdoing, and there are different types of *mens rea*, some reflecting more blameworthiness or culpability than the others.

✅ *Looking for extra marks?*

The leading textbooks examine in depth the role *mens rea* plays in attributing fault. You should read this topic in at least one of the textbooks, and in particular, we recommend:

• A Ashworth and J Horder, *Principles of Criminal Law*, OUP, 7th edn, 2013, and

• D Ormerod, *Smith and Hogan Criminal Law*, OUP, 13th edn, 2011.

Subjectivism and objectivism

Mens rea is often classified as being either **subjective** or **objective**. Put simply, any *mens rea* which is assessed subjectively is assessed by the fact-finder (the jury or magistrate(s)) according to what D was thinking at the time of the *actus reus*. An objective *mens rea* is also one which assesses what D was thinking, but in addition, the fact-finder must consider what a reasonable person would have thought, and where D did not think in the way a reasonable person would have done, the *mens rea* may be satisfied.

Which *mens rea* words are assessed subjectively and which are assessed objectively?

Subjectively

• Intention, *Moloney* [1985]

• Recklessness, *Cunningham* [1957], *R v G* [2004]

• Wilful, *Sheppard* [1980]

• Awareness, see Law Commission, *Murder, Manslaughter and Infanticide* (Law Com 304, 2006)

Objectively

• Recklessness (from 1981 to 2003 only), *Caldwell* [1982]

• Negligence (including gross negligence), *Adomako* [1994]

Intention
****

- Dishonesty, *Ghosh* [1982] (although a test of dishonesty does have a subjective element, it is a subjective assessment of an objective test. See chapter 11)

How to explain subjective and objective states of mind

Once you grasp which *mens rea* is subjective and which is objective, you must express yourself correctly. The chart in Table 3.1 should assist.

Table 3.1 Subjective and objective states of mind

Subjective (*the exact term to be used will depend on the* **mens rea** *of the crime in question*)	Objective (*the exact term to be used will depend on the* **mens rea** *of the crime in question*)
Did D intend the result? Did D realise, recognise, want, or aim to achieve the result? Did D foresee the result?	Should D have thought about the consequences of his acts? Would a reasonable person have thought about what might happen, and D is at fault for not thinking about it?
Note: express it from D's point of view. It is not OK to say D *should* have thought about …	Note: express it from the reasonable person's point of view. It is OK to say D *should* have thought about …

Intention

Widely regarded as the most important form of *mens rea*, the meaning of this word has, perhaps surprisingly, occupied much judicial time. Traditionally, intention has been split into two types; direct and indirect. Direct intention is where D acts deliberately, wanting or desiring the outcome (*Mohan* (1975)). Indirect intention (also known as oblique intention), on the other hand, usually describes the situation in which D foresees the result but does not necessarily desire it.

Two issues have confronted the judiciary. The first is how much foresight is needed before intention can be found (see Table 3.2).

Table 3.2 The degree of foresight

Case/statute	Key point
DPP v Smith [1961]	D is *presumed* to intend or foresee the natural consequences of his actions.
Criminal Justice Act 1967 s 8	Repealed the decision in *Smith* (above). The jury is not bound in law to infer intent or foresight, but is to draw inferences from the evidence.

Table 3.2 (*Continued*)

Case/statute	Key point
Hyam [1975]	The *mens rea* for murder is satisfied if D knew death or serious harm was highly probable.
Moloney [1985]	Intent could be inferred where the defendant foresaw the consequence as a natural consequence of his act.
Hancock and Shankland [1986]	The greater the probability of a consequence the more likely it was that the consequence was foreseen and the greater the probability was that that consequence was also intended.
Nedrick (1986)	Introduced the 'foresight of a virtual certainty' test, approved in *Woollin*.
Woollin [1999]	The jury is not entitled to find the necessary intention unless it feels sure that death or serious bodily harm was a virtual certainty, barring some unforeseen intervention, as a result of the accused's actions and that the accused appreciated such was the case.

The second issue is whether foresight is evidence of intention, or whether foresight of a virtual certainty is, in law, the same thing as intention (see Figure 3.1).

Does it matter whether it is law or fact?

Figure 3.1 Does it matter if law or fact?

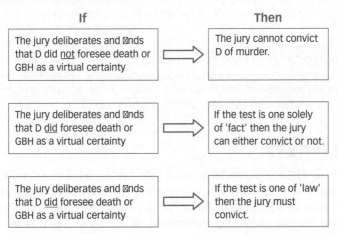

If	Then
The jury deliberates and finds that D did **not** foresee death or GBH as a virtual certainty	The jury cannot convict D of murder.
The jury deliberates and finds that D **did** foresee death or GBH as a virtual certainty	If the test is one solely of 'fact' then the jury can either convict or not.
The jury deliberates and finds that D **did** foresee death or GBH as a virtual certainty	If the test is one of 'law' then the jury must convict.

Recklessness

Is it law or fact?

The judiciary has not been consistent in answering this question. From Table 3.3, you will see that in some cases, their Lordships have said the question of whether foresight of intention is one of fact, but in other cases (and sometimes even in the same case), they also seem to treat the question as one of law.

Table 3.3 Is intention a question of fact or law?

Is it law or fact?	Case
FACT Foresight is evidence from which an inference of intent may be made by the jury; it is not equivalent to intent.	*Moloney* [1985]
LAW If the jury inferred D foresaw the result as a virtual certainty (which it does by considering all the evidence) Lord Lane said 'the inference may be irresistible that D intended that result'.	*Nedrick* (1986)
FACT Lord Lane's comment quoted above was expressly rejected, and the House of Lords emphasised intention was a matter for the jury, but LAW Lord Steyn also said 'a result foreseen as a virtual certainty is an intended result'.	*Woollin* [1999]
LAW If the doctor foresaw that death was virtually certain, the doctor intended to kill. This is a civil case and we deal with it in more detail in chapter 15.	*Re A* [2001]
FACT Although there is very little difference between a rule of evidence and one of law, foresight of a virtual certainty is evidence from which the jury may find intention.	*Matthews and Alleyne* [2003]

✅ *Looking for extra marks?*

There is academic argument about this issue. Among your reading, you might include the article by Alan Norrie (see 'Key debates' on p 39) and the exchange of letters in the *Criminal Law Review*: 'Intention and Foresight of Virtual Certainty' [1999] Crim LR 246.

Recklessness

To be reckless is to take an unjustifiable risk. A defendant is therefore not reckless if he took a justifiable risk. The justifiability of the risk is assessed objectively, ie would the reasonable man regard taking the risk as unjustifiable? If the risk was objectively justifiable, D is not reckless. If the risk was objectively unjustifiable, then the next step is to ask whether the recklessness is assessed subjectively or objectively.

Subjective recklessness

D can be convicted only where the prosecution can prove D foresaw the risk of the prohibited result (according to the definition of the offence) and nevertheless took the risk. It is sometimes referred to as advertent or conscious risk taking.

Cunningham [1957] 2 QB 396

This is the leading case. D stole a gas meter and its contents from the cellar of a house and in so doing fractured a gas pipe. The gas escaped and V inhaled a considerable quantity of the gas. D was charged with maliciously causing another to take a noxious thing under **s 23 Offences Against the Person Act 1861**. The judge directed the jury that 'maliciously' meant 'wickedly'— doing 'something which he has no business to do and perfectly well knows it'. However, D's appeal was allowed. Wherever the word 'maliciously' appears in a statutory crime, the prosecution must prove either that D intended to do the particular type of harm in fact done, or that D foresaw that such harm might be done.

Objective recklessness

By the authority of *Caldwell* [1982] (see 'Key cases' on p 37), D could have been convicted of criminal damage if the prosecution could prove D failed to consider a risk which would have been obvious to the reasonable person. *Caldwell* was overruled in *R v G* [2004], also in 'Key cases' on p 38, in which Lord Bingham opined that, 'It is clearly blameworthy to take an obvious and significant risk of causing injury to another. But it is not clearly blameworthy to do something involving a risk of injury to another if ... one genuinely does not perceive the risk. Such a person may fairly be accused of stupidity or lack of imagination, but neither of those failings should expose him to conviction of serious crime or the risk of punishment ... It is neither moral nor just to convict a defendant (least of all a child) on the strength of what someone else would have apprehended if the defendant himself had no such apprehension.'

The House of Lords adopted the Law Commission's recommendation, holding that a person acts recklessly within the meaning of **s 1 Criminal Damage Act 1971** with respect to (i) a circumstance when he is aware of a risk that it exists or will exist; (ii) a result when he is aware of a risk that it will occur; and it is, in the circumstances known to him, unreasonable to take the risk.

Negligence

Negligence is a civil concept. If D's conduct falls below the standard of a reasonable person, he is negligent. The criminal law bases liability for some minor crimes on negligence (eg driving without due care) and it also forms the basis of the more serious crime of gross negligence manslaughter (see chapter 8). Negligence can sometimes provide a statutory defence (where proof is often reversed, so that D has to prove that he was not negligent).

Coincidence of *actus reus* and *mens rea*

If the *mens rea* is formed, but the *actus reus* is not completed until later, and at a time when D no longer necessarily satisfies the *mens rea*, can D nevertheless be convicted? The answer is 'yes'.

Meli [1954] 1 WLR 228

Two defendants lured V to a hut. They hit V over the head, intending to kill him, but only knocked him unconscious. Believing he was dead, and in an effort to fake an accident, they rolled him off a cliff. V died of exposure at the bottom of the cliff. The Privy Council held 'it was impossible to divide up what was really one series of acts … '. They were therefore held to be guilty of murder.

Church [1966] 1 QB 59

D beat a woman unconscious and, in a panic and thinking she was dead, threw her into a river. At the time she was alive but then died from drowning. The Court of Appeal held that D's 'behaviour from the moment he first struck her to the moment when he threw her into the river [was] a series of acts designed to cause death …'. Even if the ultimate and fatal act is accidental, liability can be still found, as shown in *Le Brun* [1992]. D hit his wife on the chin intending serious harm and knocking her unconscious. While he was trying to drag her body along the street to avoid detection, he accidentally lost his grip. Her head hit the pavement, fracturing her skull and causing her death. The time lag between the intentional strike and V's death did not stop there being a single sequence of events.

> ✅ *Looking for extra marks?*
>
> The Court of Appeal in *Le Brun* [1992] recognised that an alternative way of solving the coincidence problem was by applying the normal principles of causation we have explained in chapter 2. Do you agree? Can you illustrate this view by example?

Transferred malice

In a case of 'transferred malice' the situation is that D aims to kill or injure X but accidentally misses and kills or injures 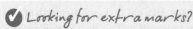 V instead. The law allows the *mens rea* to transfer to the *actus reus* against his unintended victim. In *Gnango* [2012], an innocent passer-by was accidentally shot during a shoot-out in a public place. D was convicted of her murder even though he did not fire the fatal shot. He was part of a joint criminal enterprise with a third party who did (see chapter 10).

Latimer (1886) 17 QBD 359

D went to hit X with her belt, but the belt accidentally rebounded and hit V, causing injury. D's malicious intent against X was transferred to V. However, the doctrine cannot extend to a transfer of malice from an unborn foetus to the human being the foetus is to become, nor from the mother to the unborn child. In *Attorney-General's Reference (No 3 of 1994)* [1998], D stabbed a woman (V1) in the abdomen, knowing her to be pregnant. Two weeks after the stabbing, V1 went into labour and gave birth to a premature child (V2), who was born alive but later died. On the death of V2, D was charged with V2's murder. It was held that *mens rea* could not be transferred from the mother (V1) to the foetus and then from the foetus to the child (V2). See 'Key debates' on p 40.

Further, the doctrine cannot join the *actus reus* of an offence against property, such as criminal damage (breaking a window) with the *mens rea* of an offence against the person (intention to injure V).

Pembliton (1874) LR 2 CCR 119

D had been fighting with others. He threw a stone at them, which struck a window and did damage. His intention to injure was not sufficient *mens rea* for damage to the window.

 **Key cases**

Case	Facts	Principle
Caldwell [1982] AC 341	D set fire to a hotel where he had been employed. He was so drunk at the time that it did not occur to him that there might be people there whose lives might be endangered.	The House of Lords held that a person is reckless as to whether or not any property would be destroyed or damaged if he does an act which creates an obvious risk that property will be destroyed or damaged and when he does the act he either has not given any thought to the possibility of there being any such risk; or has recognised that there was some risk involved and has nonetheless gone on to do it.
Cunningham [1957] 2 QB 396	D stole a gas meter and its contents from the cellar of a house and in so doing fractured a gas pipe. The gas escaped and V inhaled a considerable quantity of the gas. D was charged with maliciously causing another to take a noxious thing under **s 23 Offences Against the Person Act 1861**.	Wherever the word 'maliciously' appears in a statutory crime, the prosecution must prove either that D intended to do the particular type of harm in fact done, or that D foresaw that such harm might be done.

Key cases
✱✱✱✱✱✱✱✱✱✱✱

Case	Facts	Principle
Matthews and Alleyne [2003] 2 Cr App R 30	The defendants attempted to rob V and then threw him from a bridge into a river, causing his death. V had told them he could not swim. The defendants either had the intent to kill when they threw V off the bridge, or they formed that intent when, having the opportunity to save him, they failed to do so.	The Court of Appeal recognised that acting deliberately with the appreciation of a virtual certainty of death did not necessarily amount to an intention to kill, but it was evidence from which intent to kill could be inferred. On facts such as these, there is very little to choose between a rule of evidence and one of substantive law.
Moloney [1985] AC 905	D, a soldier, had been drinking heavily with his stepfather, V, all evening and V had boasted he could 'outshoot, outload and outdraw' D. D loaded two shotguns, fired one, and the bullet hit V who was six feet away. D told the police, 'I did not aim the gun. I just pulled the trigger and he was dead.'	The House of Lords laid down guidelines on what constituted the necessary mental element in murder. The judge should avoid any elaboration or paraphrase of what is meant by intent, and leave it to the jury's good sense to decide. Where, however, a direction was needed, the judge should invite the jury to consider two questions. First, was death or really serious injury a natural consequence of the defendant's voluntary act? Secondly, did the defendant foresee that consequence as being a natural consequence of his act? The jury should then be told that if they answer yes to both questions it is a proper inference for them to draw that he intended that consequence. Foresight of consequences belongs not to the substantive law, but to the law of evidence.
R v G [2004] 1 AC 1034	Two boys, aged 11 and 12, set fire to newspapers in the yard at the back of a shop and threw the lit newspapers under a wheelie bin. They left the yard without putting out the fire. The burning newspapers set fire to the bin, spread to the shop and caused £1m damage. They expected the newspapers to burn themselves out on the concrete floor of the yard and it was accepted that neither of them appreciated the risk of the fire spreading in the way that it did. The trial judge had directed the jury in accordance with the objective test given in *Caldwell*.	The House of Lords held that a person acts recklessly within the meaning of **s 1 Criminal Damage Act 1971** with respect to (i) a circumstance when he is aware of a risk that it exists or will exist; (ii) a result when he is aware of a risk that it will occur; and it is, in the circumstances known to him, unreasonable to take the risk.

Case	Facts	Principle
Woollin [1999] 1 AC 82	D lost his temper and threw his three-month-old son onto a hard surface. The child sustained a fractured skull and died, and D was charged with murder.	Where D is charged with murder and the simple direction (that it is for the jury to decide whether D intended to kill or do serious bodily harm) is not enough, the jury should be directed that they are not entitled to find the necessary intention unless they feel sure that death or serious bodily harm was a virtual certainty (barring some unforeseen intervention) as a result of D's actions and that D appreciated that was the case, the decision being one for them to reach on a consideration of all the evidence.

The key cases on the coincidence of *actus reus* and *mens rea* are *Meli* [1954], *Church* [1966], and *Le Brun* [1992], which can be found on p 36, 'Coincidence of *actus reus* and *mens rea*'.

The key cases on transferred malice are *Latimer* (1886), *Attorney-General's Reference (No 3 of 1994)* [1998], and *Pembliton* (1874), which can be found on p 37, 'Transferred malice'.

⑨ Key debates

Topic	The meaning of intention in the criminal law
Author/Academic	Alan Norrie
Viewpoint	Examines the meaning of the word intention and whether the test in *Woollin* reflected a 'moral threshold' so that even though D could foresee a result as virtually certain, it could not be conceived as a result that he intended.
Source	'After *Woollin*' [1999] Crim LR 532

For an academic analysis on the meaning of recklessness, see the 'Key debates' at the end of chapter 13.

Exam questions

Topic	**'Between orthodox subjectivism and moral contextualism: intention and the consultation paper'**
Author/Academic	Alan Norrie
Viewpoint	Examines the moral wrongness of murder, the justification for the definition of the crime (and the sentence) and the reliance on the concept of intention. Considers the relationship between offences (intention) and some defences (necessity) and the doctrine of double effect. The article should be read in light of the Law Commission's Report, *Murder, Manslaughter and Infanticide* (Law Com No 304, 2006).
Source	[2006] Crim LR 486
Topic	**'Transferred malice and the remoteness of unexpected outcomes from intention'**
Author/Academic	Jeremy Horder
Viewpoint	Examines the scope of the doctrine of transferred malice and provides a useful summary of ***Attorney-General's Reference (No 3 of 1994)***. Argues for a test of remoteness as a matter of fact, and analyses the relationship between transferred malice and causation.
Source	[2006] Crim LR 383

 (?) Exam questions

Problem question

We return to the sample question from chapter 2:

During a criminal law tutorial, an argument erupted between two students, Andrew and Mark, about the defence of insanity. Andrew picked up one of his biggest textbooks and threw it at Mark with intent to cause serious harm. Mark ducked, and the book's spine struck Kirin, another student, on her temple. Kirin fell unconscious … (the remainder of the question relates to issues examined in chapter 2).

Andrew is charged with the murder of Kirin. Discuss his criminal liability, if any.

An outline answer is included at the end of the book.

Essay question 1

Illustrating your answer with decided cases, what is the purpose of *mens rea*?

Essay question 2

The problem with the *Woollin* direction is that it fails to answer the following question: Say the jury returns after hours of deliberation and the foreman tells the judge that all members of the jury are in agreement that the death of the victim was a virtual certainty and that the defendant foresaw it as such, but that half of the jury wants to convict and half wants to acquit. What should the judge tell the jury?

Discuss.

Online Resource Centre

To see an outline answer to this question log on to www.oxfordtextbooks.co.uk/orc/concentrate/

#4
Strict liability

Key facts

- An element of the *actus reus* of an offence is 'strict liability' if that element does not have any *mens rea*.

- Strict liability is often referred to as no-fault liability.

- Strict liability is very rare at common law.

- Where a statute is silent as to *mens rea*, the judge must interpret the provision to decide if the offence has *mens rea* (the starting point) or is one of strict liability.

- There is a debate about whether the imposition of criminal liability in the absence of proof of fault can be justified.

Chapter overview

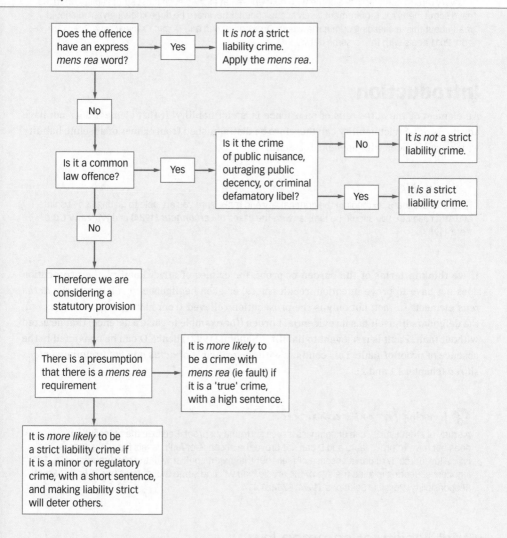

Does the offence have an express *mens rea* word? → Yes → It *is not* a strict liability crime. Apply the *mens rea*.

↓ No

Is it a common law offence? → Yes → Is it the crime of public nuisance, outraging public decency, or criminal defamatory libel? → No → It *is not* a strict liability crime.

→ Yes → It *is* a strict liability crime.

↓ No

Therefore we are considering a statutory provision

↓

There is a presumption that there is a *mens rea* requirement → It is *more likely* to be a crime with *mens rea* (ie fault) if it is a 'true' crime, with a high sentence.

↓

It is *more likely* to be a strict liability crime if it is a minor or regulatory crime, with a short sentence, and making liability strict will deter others.

Introduction

****

Introduction

An element of the *actus reus* of an offence is 'strict liability' if that element does not have any *mens rea*. Strict liability can therefore be distinguished from crimes of absolute liability which are offences with no *mens rea* at all.

If we think in terms of the burden of proof, for crimes of strict liability, the prosecution does not have to prove intention, recklessness, or even negligence in relation to the *actus reus* element. In fact, not only is the prosecution relieved from having to prove *mens rea*, the defendant himself has no evidential burden (for example to raise a defence) that he acted without fault. Fault is irrelevant to liability (Sandhu [1997]) hence D can be convicted in the absence of proof of fault. This conflicts with the principle of *actus non facit reum nisi mens sit rea* (chapters 1 and 2).

Strict liability at common law

Strict liability at common law is increasingly rare. The only remaining common law offences where liability is strict are public nuisance, outraging public decency, and the publication of a defamatory libel. Blasphemous libel, which was the publication of material likely to outrage and insult the Christian religion, an offence of strict liability, was abolished by s 79 Criminal Justice and Immigration Act 2008.

Strict liability by statute

There are hundreds of statutory strict liability crimes.

Where the statute is silent as to *mens rea*, then whether the crime is strict liability is a matter of judicial reasoning, and the reasoning involves issues of precedent (what has been decided in previous cases about these words, if anything?) and statutory interpretation. The leading case on judicial reasoning in respect of strict liability is *Gammon (Hong Kong) Ltd v Attorney-General of Hong Kong* [1985].

··

Gammon (Hong Kong) Ltd v Attorney-General of Hong Kong [1985] AC 1

The defendants were involved in the construction of a building in Hong Kong. The building collapsed and they were charged with having deviated in a material way from the plans. There was no evidence that they realised the deviation they made was material. The Privy Council, dismissing their appeals, laid out the test (summarised in 'Key cases', p 48) for judges to use when determining whether an offence imposes strict liability.

··

There is a presumption of mens rea

This means the judge's task is to presume the offence has a *mens rea* requirement and therefore if the prosecution cannot prove D had that *mens rea*, D is not guilty. See *Sweet v Parsley* [1970] and *B v DPP* [2000] in 'Key cases', pp 48–49.

The presumption is particularly strong if the offence is truly criminal

It may strike you as odd that *crimes* can be classified as *truly criminal*, and conversely therefore *not truly criminal*, but this classification generally (but not conclusively) means:

- serious crimes, those with long sentences, and/or carrying a stigma on conviction are **truly criminal** and are more likely to have *mens rea*, and

- quasi-crimes, **regulatory crimes**, minor crimes, those carrying a lighter sentence and/or no stigma on conviction are more likely to be strict liability. See *B v DPP* [2000] and *Shah* [2000] (also in 'Key cases', p 48). Refer also to *Muhamad* [2003] regarding offence seriousness and the sentence.

What is the construction of the provision?

As a matter of statutory interpretation, judges will consider the meaning of the words within the section in issue, in other sections in the same Act, in other sections in other Acts, and from the previous law (common law or statutory).

Displacing the presumption of *mens rea* can be done only if it is a necessary implication on the wording of the provision, see *B v DPP* [2000].

Issues concerning public safety and vigilance

If the crime involves public safety such as food safety, employee safety, driving and road safety, access to the emergency services and so on *and* in the court's view making the crime one of strict liability will ensure greater vigilance *and* act as a deterrent to others *then* even if the crime is 'truly' criminal, it can be a strict liability offence (see *Blake* [1997]).

Revision tip

Bear in mind, the *Gammon* test is straightforward to recite, but it is not so easy to apply. It is not a quantitative assessment (where we simply add up the factors on each side and conclude) but a qualitative assessment of the value of each factor in order to reach a decision.

The relationship between strict liability and mistake

Mistake is a full defence which may result in an acquittal. We call it a defence, but it is an assertion by the defendant that he did not form *mens rea*. The burden of proof in relation to mistake actually lies on the prosecution (that is, to prove that D did form *mens rea*). Because mistake negates *mens rea*, it follows as a matter of logic that mistake cannot be a defence for crimes of strict liability. Historically, the best case to illustrate this principle is *Prince* (1875).

Revision tip

Prince (1875) used to be used to illustrate two principles:

1. The age element of age-based crimes, such as sexual offences against child victims, was strict liability. In light of the decision in *B v DPP* [2000] ('Key cases', p 48), *this is no longer necessarily good law in all cases*.
2. Mistake is no defence, even if the mistake is reasonable, to strict liability crimes. This is still an accurate representation of the law.

....

Prince (1875) LR 2 CCR 154

D was charged with taking an unmarried girl under the age of 16 out of the possession of her father against his will. D knew the girl was under the possession of her father, but reasonably believed she was 18. She was in fact under 16. The court held the offence was strict as to age so D's mistake as to her age was irrelevant, despite the fact that it was reasonable.

....

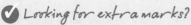

✅ Looking for extra marks?

In *Tolson* (1889) D's genuine and reasonable mistake about her husband's death was a defence on a charge of bigamy even though the offence is one of strict liability. This outcome appears to conflict with *Prince* above. Your analysis of this conflict might be useful in an essay question on the law governing mistake and strict liability, or even a problem question where the facts lead you to apply the law to a mistake made by D.

Can strict liability be justified?

No:

- Strict liability breaches human rights. Although a conviction in the absence of proof of fault does not necessarily violate the presumption of innocence under Article 6 (see *Salabiaku* (1991) and *G v UK* (2011)), the imposition of strict liability *may* breach Article 7 (certainty in the criminal law) where the courts have not yet determined whether a particular crime is of strict liability (see *Muhamad* [2003]).

- Strict liability is harsh; it allows a defendant to be convicted even though there was nothing at all he could have done to comply with the law (see for example *Callow v Tillstone* (1900)).

- Reasonable errors, and those made in good faith and without negligence, do not relieve D of liability.

- There is no common law no-negligence/due diligence defence, and the use of the defence in Acts of Parliament is haphazard to say the least.

Yes:

- The criminal law is designed to prevent harmful acts. Crimes of strict liability fulfil that function.

- Ease of proof.

- Deterrent effect.

Key cases

✳✳✳✳✳✳✳✳✳✳

Revision tip

Questions on strict liability are commonly essay questions which ask you to consider whether criminal liability in the absence of fault can be justified. You should make sure you have read a leading textbook on this, and make sure you are able to illustrate your answer with a full range of cases. See also 'Key debates' at the end of this chapter.

(✳) Key cases

Case	Facts	Principle
B v DPP [2000] 2 AC 428	D, a boy aged 15, repeatedly asked a 13-year-old girl to perform oral sex during a bus journey. He was convicted of inciting a girl under the age of 14 to commit an act of gross indecency. D said he honestly believed that the girl was over 14.	The House of Lords held it was not necessary to displace the presumption of *mens rea*, nor was it 'compellingly clear' that Parliament intended liability to be strict. The *mens rea* was lack of an honest belief that the complainant was aged 14 or over.
Gammon (Hong Kong) Ltd v Attorney-General of Hong Kong [1985] AC 1	The defendants were involved in the construction of a building in Hong Kong. The building collapsed and they were charged with having deviated in a material way from the plans. There was no evidence that they realised the deviation they made was material.	The Privy Council laid out the test for judges to use when determining whether an offence imposes strict liability. First, there is a presumption of law that *mens rea* is required before a person can be held guilty of a criminal offence and that presumption is particularly strong where the offence is 'truly criminal' in character. The presumption can be displaced only if this is clearly or by necessary implication the effect of the statute and only where the offence is concerned with an issue of social concern. However, even where a statute is concerned with such an issue, the presumption of *mens rea* stands unless it can also be shown that the creation of strict liability will be effective to promote the object of the statute by encouraging greater vigilance to prevent the commission of the prohibited act.
Harrow London Borough Council v Shah [2000] 1 WLR 83	The Ds were newsagents. One of their employees sold a lottery ticket to a boy aged 13½. The Ds were charged with offences relating to selling lottery tickets to persons under 16.	The offences were strict liability: 1. Other sections of the Act provided a defence of due diligence, but this section did not. 2. The offence was plainly not truly criminal in character. 3. The legislation dealt with an issue of social concern, namely, gambling among young people.

Case	Facts	Principle
Sweet v Parsley [1970] AC 132	D had been convicted of managing premises where cannabis was used. D was a teacher. She sublet a house to students. She did not know the students had been smoking cannabis.	Her appeal was allowed by the House of Lords. If a section is silent as to *mens rea* there is a presumption that, in order to give effect to the will of Parliament, judges must read in words appropriate to require *mens rea*.

Key debates

Topic	Can strict liability be justified, and if so when and why?
Author/Academic	Jeremy Horder
Viewpoint	Examines the distinction between 'true' and regulatory crimes, giving examples of the activities which have been regulated through strict liability. Considers whether the regulation of intrinsically useful activities by strict liability is desirable and criticises the under-use of negligence as a suitable alternative to no-fault liability.
Source	'Strict liability, statutory construction and the spirit of liberty' (2002) 118 LQR 458

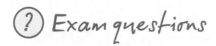

Exam questions

Problem question

Alex was the landlord of a pub. One night, after the pub closed, one of Alex's customers, Bert, was arrested by police after he left the pub, for an offence of being drunk in a public place. Bert pleaded guilty to the offence, but said that Alex had served him the alcohol. The police then arrested Alex for selling alcohol to a person who is drunk, contrary to **s 141 Licensing Act 2003** which provides that a person commits an offence if he knowingly sells alcohol to a person who is drunk. Alex remembers selling Bert several alcoholic drinks but it was a busy night in the pub, and Alex did not consider whether Bert was drunk or not.

Critically consider whether the words 'a person who is drunk' in **s 141 Licensing Act 2003** are strict liability.

An outline answer is included at the end of the book.

Exam questions

✱✱✱✱✱✱✱✱✱✱

Essay question

The imposition of strict liability cannot be justified. The risk is too high that the blameless may be convicted.

Discuss.

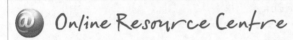

Online Resource Centre

To see an outline answer to this question log on to www.oxfordtextbooks.co.uk/orc/concentrate/

#5
Non-fatal offences against the person

Key facts

- There are five principal offences examined in this chapter, namely **assault** and **battery** (the common assaults) and the offences under **ss 47, 20, and 18 Offences Against the Person Act 1861** (referred to as the **OAPA**).

- There are many other non-fatal offences against the person (for example poisoning, gassing) but they do not feature on most criminal law programmes, so are not covered here.

- The victim's consent may negate the offence, but whether or not it does depends to a great extent on the type of crime, what the victim knows, the extent of the harm which is caused, and matters of public policy.

- Stalking and harassment are crimes in certain circumstances.

- Four of the principal assaults are aggravated if the crime committed is motivated by religious or racial hatred.

Chapter overview

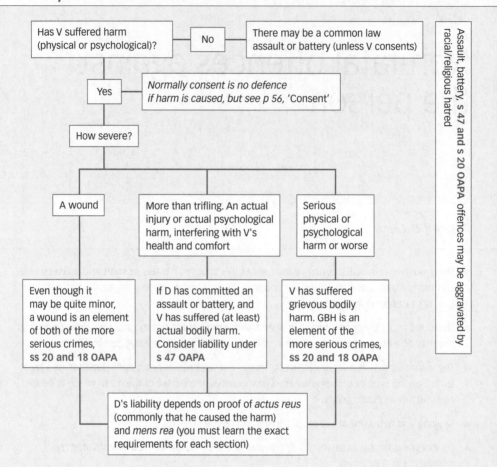

Has V suffered harm (physical or psychological)? → **No** → There may be a common law assault or battery (unless V consents)

Yes

Normally consent is no defence if harm is caused, but see p 56, 'Consent'

How severe?

A wound	More than trifling. An actual injury or actual psychological harm, interfering with V's health and comfort	Serious physical or psychological harm or worse
Even though it may be quite minor, a wound is an element of both of the more serious crimes, **ss 20 and 18 OAPA**	If D has committed an assault or battery, and V has suffered (at least) actual bodily harm. Consider liability under **s 47 OAPA**	V has suffered grievous bodily harm. GBH is an element of the more serious crimes, **ss 20 and 18 OAPA**

D's liability depends on proof of *actus reus* (commonly that he caused the harm) and *mens rea* (you must learn the exact requirements for each section)

Assault, battery, s 47 and s 20 OAPA offences may be aggravated by racial/religious hatred

Revision Tip

Tutors regularly comment on students' failure correctly to state the *actus reus* and *mens rea* of the non-fatal offences against the person. These elements are not particularly complex or challenging, but they do take time and a degree of effort to learn and understand.

Introduction

If you are hoping to do the 'non-fatals' question in the exam, when you are reading the exam question, make sure the victim is not dead. Read to the end of the question before you start writing your answer. What appears to be, say, an assault or battery might ultimately cause V's death, so if you should be considering homicide, do not start the answer with an assault.

Please also note that in this chapter, we are not examining the sexual offences which are considered in detail in chapter 6, nor are we considering offences which deal with property (see chapters 11, 12, and 13). Other than the 'defence' of consent (and why the word is in inverted commas will become clear later) we are not examining defences in this chapter either.

The law studied here is a mixture of common law and legislation. We tend to regard the five principal offences on a ladder of seriousness; with a technical assault on the bottom rung (the least serious) and an offence contrary to s 18 OAPA on the top. When we refer to offence seriousness in this context, we mean seriousness both in terms of harm caused and the *mens rea* of the offence.

Technical assault

Before we look at the definition of this offence, you should be aware that the word 'assault' features regularly in this chapter and the meaning may change according to context:

1. A technical or psychic assault which is covered on pp 53–5. This offence never involves physical contact.

2. As a collective noun encompassing the separate crimes (*DPP v Little* (1992)) of technical or psychic assault and physical assault or battery. The correct term to cover the crimes together is 'common assault'.

3. In s 47 OAPA, where the single word 'assault' has been construed to mean 'common assault'. We will examine battery and s 47 on p 55, 'Physical assault/battery' and on p 58, 'Section 47 Offences Against the Person Act 1861'.

Definitional elements of a technical assault

This is a common law offence (see *Haystead v CC of Derbyshire* [2000]). Table 5.1 summarises the elements of technical assault.

Technical assault

✳✳✳✳✳✳✳✳✳✳✳

Table 5.1 The elements of technical assault

Actus reus	Mens rea
D does an act which causes V to apprehend (expect) the immediate application of unlawful violence	D intends V to have the apprehension referred to in the *actus reus*, or D foresees (ie is reckless) V might have such an apprehension, *Venna* [1975]

Revision Tip

Assault is sometimes described as a statutory offence; why? **Section 39 Criminal Justice Act 1988** governs mode of trial and sentence, but it does not define the offence, which is one defined at common law.

Examples of technical assault include a person raising his fists to another, meaning the other is afraid that the first is going to harm him. It could also involve, say, waving a knife or a gun in a threatening manner. It does not, however, include these types of actions if the other (the 'victim') has no expectation of being harmed there and then.

....

Lamb [1967] 2 QB 981

D, in jest, pointed a revolver at V, who joined in the game. The revolver had five chambers, in two of which were live bullets, neither of which was in the chamber opposite the barrel when D pulled the trigger. The chamber rotated before firing, a bullet was struck by the striking pin and V, D's friend, was killed. The Court of Appeal held that the prosecution had been unable to prove D had the *mens rea* for assault (intention or recklessness to cause V to apprehend immediate unlawful harm). We revisit this case in chapter 8 when we examine unlawful act manslaughter ('Unlawful act manslaughter', p 101).

....

The main issues

- Words alone may amount to a technical assault (*Constanza* [1997], see 'Key cases', p 66).
- Words may negate what would otherwise be an assault (*Tuberville v Savage* (1669)).
- Silence may amount to an assault (*Ireland* [1998]).
- Immediate does not necessarily mean instantaneously (*Smith v Superintendent of Woking Police* (1983). See also *Ireland* [1998]).
- Apprehend does not mean fear. It means expect. The victim may be in fear, but V does not have to be afraid for there to be an expectation. However, if V does not expect to be harmed, there is no technical assault (*Lamb* (1967)).

Avoiding common mistakes

The most common mistakes students make when explaining or applying the law on technical assault are:

- confusing fear with apprehension (see 'The main issues', above, p 54);
- confusing an immediate apprehension with an apprehension of immediate harm, so:
  - if V says 'I now expect to be hit later', there is no technical assault (even if V is very afraid of the future harm), but
  - if V says 'I expect now to be hit now, but I am not afraid', the *actus reus* of a technical assault is satisfied. Do not forget to consider if D satisfies the *mens rea* too.

Physical assault/battery

A physical assault, also known as a battery, is an act or omission which always involves physical contact between D and V (although it might be indirect), but it does not necessarily include any harm to V.

> *Revision tip*
> If harm is caused you should be considering an offence under the **OAPA** instead of, or as well as, a battery.

The usual example of a battery is where D hits V, but a commonly cited example is an unwanted kiss. ✓

Definitional elements of a battery

Table 5.2 summarises the elements of battery.

Table 5.2 The elements of battery

Actus reus	Mens rea
D applies unlawful force to V	D intends to apply unlawful force, or D foresees (ie D is reckless) that he might apply unlawful force

The main issues

- Any unlawful touching may be a battery (*Thomas* (1985)).
- There need not be an injury for there to be a battery, but very minor injuries are often charged as batteries rather than one of the statutory crimes (see the CPS *Charging Standards* (which do not have legal effect)).

Physical assault/battery

- It is possible to commit a battery indirectly (see 'Key debates' on p 67 and *Haystead v Chief Constable of Derbyshire* [2000]).
- It is possible to commit a battery by omission (*DPP v K* [1990], *DPP v Santana-Bermudez* [2004], cf *Fagan* [1968]).   *needles*

Policeman fool

Consent

Consent is a defence to assault and battery, but may be a defence to the more serious statutory crimes (see p 58 onwards) only in certain situations, so it is useful to consider the defence at this stage. The best way to tackle the complex issues which arise here (given the compact nature of this book) is to ask and answer a few fundamental questions:

When is consent a 'defence'?

V's consent, that is his or her agreement or willingness to have physical contact with D, will usually mean that the physical contact between them is not a crime. However, V's consent must be valid and the law does not always allow people, even adults, to give valid consent (even if they might in fact consent).

Why is the word 'defence' in inverted commas?

If you think about what has to be proved, in all crimes of violence, the prosecution must prove that the contact was unlawful. If V consented to the contact, it is, by definition, not unlawful. Consent is therefore not a defence insofar as D has to prove it, or insofar as the *actus reus* and *mens rea* can be established independently but then liability is excused because of V's consent. Rather, consent negates the unlawfulness of the conduct and therefore there is no *actus reus*.

> ✔ **Looking for extra marks?**
>
> The view expressed that consent negates the *actus reus* is the prevailing view (see *B v DPP* [2000] and *Kimber* [1983]), and *obiter dicta* to the contrary in *Brown* [1994] is generally regarded as not surviving the later decision. Can you explain this in your own words?

Are we dealing with a crime of violence?

If we are, then V cannot give valid consent where actual bodily harm is intended and/or caused unless it is in the public interest; see *Brown* [1994].

⋯⋯⋯

Brown [1994] 1 AC 212

The defendants were a group of sado-masochists, who willingly and enthusiastically participated in the commission of acts of violence against each other for the sexual pleasure it engendered in the giving and receiving of pain. However, the House of Lords held that it is not in the public interest that a person should wound or cause actual bodily harm to another for no good reason and, in the absence of such a reason, the victim's consent afforded no defence to a charge under s 20 or s 47 OAPA. The satisfying of sado-masochistic desires did not constitute such a good reason.

....

Be very careful to identify correctly if it is a crime of violence or not. In *Wilson* [1997], branding V's skin was not a crime of violence as there was no aggressive intent; see also *Slingsby* [1995]. Sado-masochistic acts are crimes of violence (see *Brown* [1994] and also *Emmett* (1999)).

If V can consent to acts of violence in the public interest, what is in the public interest?

Examples include:

- boxing and other contact sports such as rugby;
- tattooing;
- ear piercing; and
- circumcision (male).

✔ Looking for extra marks?

Read the majority and the minority opinions in *Brown* [1994]. You are looking for where the line is drawn between violent acts which are in the public interest and those which are not. You might want to think about the role of the criminal law too. Does the criminal law have a place in the private sexual acts of consenting adults? See 'Key debates', p 67 for analysis and evaluation of the leading cases.

Is messing around (horseplay) in the public interest?

The Court of Appeal has held that consent to injuries suffered in 'rough and undisciplined' horseplay is something that must be left to the jury's consideration.

....

Jones [1987] Crim LR 123

V suffered GBH after having been thrown in the air by D, a school friend, in a playground incident. The Court of Appeal thought that the jury might have rejected the defence of consent, but the judge should have allowed the jury to consider it. Very serious injuries were caused to V in *Aitken* [1992] when two RAF officers set fire to V's fire resistant suit, but as V had previously taken part in the horseplay, it was possible that his continued presence was an acceptance by him that such an activity might be perpetrated on him and an indication that he consented to it.

....

A similar decision was reached in *Richardson and Irwin* [1999], which we will consider in chapter 14.

If it is not a crime of violence, when can V give valid consent?

The law governing consent to non-violent crime focuses not on the extent of the harm, but on the victim's knowledge and understanding of the nature and quality of the act.

....

Tabassum [2000] 2 Cr App R 328

D asked several women to take part in what he said was a breast cancer survey and this involved allowing D to feel their breasts. The women said that they had only consented because they thought D had either medical qualifications or relevant training, and he had neither. The Court of Appeal dismissed his appeal against conviction, holding that there was no true consent since the women were consenting to touching for medical purposes. They therefore consented to the nature of the act but not to its quality.

....

The decision in *Tabassum* was approved in *Dica* [2004], which is explained in 'Key cases', p 66, and between them these two cases have rendered the old decision in *Clarence* (1888) obsolete on the consent issue. In *Clarence*, the wife's consent to sexual intercourse not knowing her husband had gonorrhoea was a defence.

✅ *Looking for extra marks?*

Strictly, not all of the judgment in *Clarence* (1888) has been overruled. Once you have completed this chapter, *and* understand the definitional elements of **s 20** at 'Section 20 Offences Against the Person Act 1861', p 60, can you explain, precisely, what the effect of the later cases might be on *Clarence*? Hint, you might find some answers in paras [30] and [31] of *Dica*, per Judge LJ. Might *Clarence* still be good law for the meaning of inflict where there is a *physical* injury?

Section 47 Offences Against the Person Act 1861

Whosoever shall be convicted ... of any assault occasioning actual bodily harm shall be liable ...

Definitional elements of an offence under s 47

Think of a s 47 offence as an aggravated assault or an aggravated battery, as depicted in Figure 5.1.

The harm which must result from the assault or battery must amount to **actual bodily harm**, which means any hurt or injury calculated to interfere with the health and comfort of V (*Miller* [1954]) and whilst it may include psychiatric harm (*Ireland* [1998]) it does not include mere emotions such as fear or panic, or states of mind which are less than an identifiable clinical condition (*Chan Fook* [1994]). The elements of s 47 OAPA are summarised in Table 5.3.

Figure 5.1 Section 47 as an aggravated assault

| Either | assault | which causes | actual harm | = | Section 47 |

| Or | battery | which causes | actual harm | = | Section 47 |

Table 5.3 The elements of a section 47 offence

jumping from the Car.

Actus reus	Mens rea
• 'Assault' (which can be either a technical assault or a battery or both)	• If the 'assault' is a technical assault, the prosecution has to prove the *mens rea* of a technical assault or
• Occasioning (which simply means causing, see *Roberts* (1971) on p 23 in chapter 2)	• If the 'assault' is battery, the prosecution has to prove the *mens rea* of a battery
• Actual bodily harm (ABH)	

....

Ireland [1998] AC 147

D made a large number of telephone calls to three women and remained silent when they answered. A psychiatrist who examined the women stated that as a result of the repeated telephone calls each of them had suffered psychological damage. D appealed against his convictions for offences contrary to s 47 on the basis that silence cannot amount to an assault, and psychological damage is not bodily harm. The House of Lords dismissed his appeal. Where the making of a silent telephone call caused fear of immediate and unlawful violence, the caller would be guilty of an assault, if he formed *mens rea*, and recognisable psychiatric illnesses were capable of falling within the phrase 'bodily harm'.

....

The main issues

- Psychiatric harm may be bodily harm, that is ABH or even GBH if serious enough: *Miller* [1954], *Chan Fook* [1994], and *Ireland* [1998].

- Liability for a s 47 offence is constructive. This means liability for the more serious offence is built out of, or constructed from, liability for a lesser offence (the assault or battery) but without any additional *mens rea* in respect of the more serious elements (the harm), see *Savage* [1992].

- By implication, therefore, there is no *mens rea* with regard to the causing of harm, see *Savage* [1992].

✱✱✱✱✱✱✱✱✱✱

Savage [1992] 1 AC 699

D threw the contents of a glass of beer over V and as she did so, the glass broke and cut V. On appeal, her conviction for a s 20 offence (considered below, p 60, 'Section 20 Offences Against the Person Act 1861') was substituted with a conviction for a s 47 offence; the s 20 offence requires the prosecution to prove D foresaw some harm to V, but the s 47 offence does not. The prosecution must simply prove the *mens rea* of a technical assault or (as here) a battery.

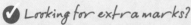 **Looking for extra marks?**

See R Stone, 'Reckless Assaults after Savage and Parmenter' OJLS 578 for a further insight into these offences.

Avoiding common mistakes

- Do not confuse the *mens rea* for a battery (as to *contact*) with the *harm* caused for a s 47 offence, as to which there is no *mens rea*. Take your time to think about this and understand it.
- Do not call the offence 'ABH'. It is an offence contrary to s 47 OAPA and consists of an assault which occasions ABH. If you use a shorthand term, you (i) misrepresent the law and (ii) could forget the assault and the causation issues.
- Do not overstate the *mens rea*:
  - X ~~Intending or being reckless as to the occasioning of actual bodily harm.~~
  - √ Intending or being reckless as to causing V to apprehend the immediate application of unlawful force (assault) or intending or being reckless as to the application of unlawful force (battery).

Section 20 Offences Against the Person Act 1861

Whosoever shall unlawfully and maliciously wound or inflict any grievous bodily harm upon any other person, either with or without any weapon or instrument, shall be guilty …

Revision tip

If you are permitted to take a statute book into the exam *do not copy the section* out in full—the examiner will not give you credit for copying! *Extract* the information—the *actus reus* and *mens rea* as shown in the boxes in Table 5.4.

Definitional elements of an offence under s 20

Table 5.4 The elements of a section 20 offence

Actus reus	Mens rea
D unlawfully **wounds** or unlawfully inflicts **grievous bodily harm** (GBH)	'Maliciously', which means intentionally or recklessly (*Cunningham* [1957]), and in this context it means intending or foreseeing some harm (*Mowatt* [1968], approved in *Savage* [1992])

There are two ways of committing a s 20 offence:

- Maliciously wounding
- Maliciously inflicting GBH

A wound consists of the breaking of both layers of the skin (the dermis and epidermis, *JJC v Eisenhower* (1984)). Usually in the exam you will be told V has a cut or laceration. GBH means 'really serious harm' (*DPP v Smith* [1961]) but the jury can be instructed in terms of 'serious' harm (*Saunders* [1985]). The CPS *Charging Standards* suggest that it is GBH where there is:

- a substantial loss of blood, usually necessitating a transfusion;
- lengthy treatment or incapacity;
- permanent disability or permanent loss of sensory function;
- permanent, visible disfigurement;
- broken or displaced limbs or bones, including fractured skull;
- broken cheek bone, jaw, ribs, etc.

Revision tip

Injuries do not have to be permanent to be GBH, but serious permanent injuries will be GBH.
    Wounding and GBH are alternatives (wound *or* GBH). Wounds do not have to be serious/GBH.

✅ *Looking for extra marks?*

What seems to be injury amounting to ABH can actually be GBH where the victim is very young (or perhaps even unusually vulnerable). See *Bolam* [2004]. This might be important for you to notice in a problem question, subject to the facts of the question.

The main issues

- To inflict was traditionally interpreted to be narrower than to cause (s 18) but no longer seems to involve the direct application of force, not where the harm is psychiatric at least (*Burstow* [1998]).

- If serious enough, psychiatric harm may be GBH (*Burstow* [1998]).

- The *mens rea* does not correspond to the *actus reus*. The prosecution does not have to prove D intended the wound or intended the GBH, or even foresaw the wound or the GBH. It is enough for the prosecution to prove D foresaw some harm (*Mowatt* [1968]).

....

Burstow [1998] AC 147

D conducted a campaign of harassment of a woman with whom he had previously had a relationship. He made silent telephone calls, distributed offensive cards in the street where she lived, sent menacing notes to her, appeared at her home and place of work and took photographs of her and her family. A consultant psychiatrist stated that she was suffering from a severe depressive illness. He appealed against his conviction under s 20 on the basis that depressive illness is not bodily harm and harm cannot be inflicted indirectly. The House of Lords dismissed his appeal. On the meaning of bodily harm, see *Ireland* [1998] at p 59; inflict does not mean that whatever causes the harm has to be applied directly to V.

....

Avoiding common mistakes

- Do not overstate the *mens rea*:
    - X ~~Intention to wound or intention to inflict GBH~~
    - √ Foreseeing (or intending) some harm

Section 18 Offences Against the Person Act 1861

Whosoever shall unlawfully and maliciously by any means whatsoever wound or cause any grievous bodily harm to any person, with intent to do some grievous bodily harm to any person, or with intent to resist or prevent the lawful apprehension or detainer of any person, shall be guilty ...

Definitional elements of an offence under s 18

There are four ways of committing this offence, as stated in Table 5.5.

1. Wounding with intent to cause GBH.
2. Wounding with malicious intent to resist arrest etc.

3. Causing GBH with intent to cause GBH.
4. Causing GBH with malicious intent to resist arrest etc.

Table 5.5 The elements of a section 18 offence

Actus reus	Mens rea
D unlawfully wounds or unlawfully causes grievous bodily harm (GBH) to V	D intends to cause GBH, or D foresees some harm and intends to resist lawful arrest etc

In terms of *actus reus*, the terms wound and GBH are as for the s 20 offence. 'Cause' carries the same meaning as examined in chapter 2.

For the *mens rea*, the section is a little confusing. If the prosecution is simply relying on intent to cause GBH, there is no need to prove D was malicious (malicious means the same as for s 20: foresight of some harm. So, if D intended really serious harm, he would logically have foreseen at least some harm), but if the prosecution is relying on intent to resist arrest, etc, then there must also be proof of maliciousness, ie that D foresaw some harm. Note: there is no such *mens rea* as intention to wound.

The differences between s 18 and s 20 are outlined in Table 5.6.

Table 5.6 The differences between s 18 and s 20

Section 20	Section 18
Wound	Wound
or	or
inflict GBH	cause GBH
Intent to do some harm, or foresight of some harm	Intent to do GBH, or foresight of some harm with intent to resist arrest

Revision tip

Copy out Table 5.7 and annotate it with cases and commentary to aid your revision.

Section 18 Offences Against the Person Act 1861

****

Table 5.7 Revision grid: non-fatal offences against the person

Offence	*Actus reus*	*Mens rea*	Definitions, comments, and cases
s 18 OAPA	Unlawfully wound or cause GBH	Intent to cause GBH or maliciously + with intent to resist lawful apprehension, etc …	
s 20 OAPA	Unlawfully wound or inflict GBH	Maliciously meaning?	
s 47 OAPA	Assault (either physical or technical or both) occasioning ABH	*Mens rea* as for the physical and/or technical assault	
Common/ physical assault battery	Application of unlawful force to victim	Intention or recklessness to apply unlawful force to the victim	
Common/ technical/psychic assault	Causing the victim to apprehend immediate unlawful force (harm? violence?)	Intention or recklessness to cause the victim to apprehend immediate force (etc)	

The Protection from Harassment Act 1997

- s 2 prohibits harassment (which includes alarming the person or causing the person distress, see *R (on the application of Waxman) v CPS* (2012));

- s 2A prohibits harassment by stalking (which includes, for example, following, contacting, monitoring, watching and spying on a person);

- s 4 prohibits harassment by putting people in fear of violence (*Thomas v News Group Newspapers Ltd* (2001));

- s 4A prohibits stalking involving causing serious alarm or distress, or stalking involving fear of violence,

where in each case D follows a course of conduct which D knows or a reasonable person with the same information would know would cause the other to have such alarm, distress, fear, as appropriate to each charge.

A course of conduct must be at least two incidents; whether those two, or more, amount to a 'course' is a question of fact. The fewer the number of incidents and the wider the time lapse, the less likely such a fact would be found (compare *Lau v DPP* [2000] with *Kelly v DPP* [2002]).

Racial/religious aggravation

Under the provisions of the **Crime and Disorder Act 1998**, a person who commits an assault or battery, or an offence under **ss 47 or 20 OAPA 1861**, or **ss 2 or 4 Protection from Harassment Act 1997**, where that 'base' offence is racially or religiously motivated, may receive a penalty which is more severe than that available for the offence under normal circumstances.

 *Looking for extra marks?*

For an insight into the meaning of racially aggravated, see the opinion of Baroness Hale in *Rogers* [2007].

Reform

The Ministry of Justice asked the Law Commission in 2012 to conduct a scoping exercise as the first step towards a reform of the law on offences against the person. This is expected to launch in 2014. For a brief summary of the reasons why reforms are needed, see www.lawcommission.justice.gov.uk/areas/offences-against-the-person.htm.

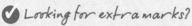 *Key cases*

Case	Facts	Principle
Brown [1994] 1 AC 212	The defendants, a group of sado-masochists, willingly and enthusiastically participated in the commission of acts of violence against each other for the sexual pleasure it engendered in the giving and receiving of pain.	It is not in the public interest that a person should wound or cause actual bodily harm to another for no good reason and, in the absence of such a reason, the victim's consent afforded no defence to a charge under **s 20** or **s 47 OAPA**; that the satisfying of sado-masochistic desires did not constitute such a good reason. This decision was upheld at the European Court of Human Rights, see **Laskey v United Kingdom** (1997) 24 EHRR 39.
Burstow [1998] AC 147, heard at the House of Lords with *Ireland*	D conducted a campaign of harassment of a woman with whom he had previously had a relationship. He made silent telephone calls, distributed offensive cards in the street where she lived, sent menacing notes to her, appeared at her home and place of work, and took photographs of her and her family.	1. On the meaning of *bodily* harm: see *Ireland*.

Key cases

****

Case	Facts	Principle
	A consultant psychiatrist stated that V was suffering from a severe depressive illness. D appealed against his conviction under **s 20** on two grounds: 1. depressive illness is not bodily harm; and 2. harm cannot be inflicted indirectly.	2. On the meaning of *inflict*: Inflict includes the infliction of psychiatric injury on another and does not mean that whatever causes the harm has to be applied directly to V. Lord Steyn held there is no radical divergence between inflict (**s 20**) and cause (**s 18**), but the words are not synonymous.
Constanza [1997] 2 Cr App R 492	D wished to form a relationship with V, who did not reciprocate. D followed V, sent her more than 800 letters, telephoned her on numerous occasions, only speaking sometimes, watched her house from his car, and wrote on her door. There was medical evidence that D's actions caused V to suffer from a clinical state of depression and anxiety. He appealed against his conviction under **s 47** on the ground that her fear of violence was not sufficiently immediate.	The Court of Appeal dismissed his appeal, holding that it was sufficient for the prosecution to prove a fear of violence at some time not excluding the immediate future. It was not essential that V was able to see the potential perpetrator of the violence, and conduct accompanying words was capable of making the words an assault.
Dica [2004] QB 1257	The defendant, knowing that he was HIV positive, had unprotected consensual sexual intercourse with two women, who were both subsequently diagnosed as HIV positive. He was charged with offences under **s 20 OAPA** on the basis that he had recklessly transmitted the disease to the women when they did not know of, and did not consent to, the risk of infection.	A person who, knowing that he is suffering a serious sexual disease, recklessly transmits it to another through consensual sexual intercourse may be guilty of inflicting grievous bodily harm, contrary to **s 20 OAPA**. V's consent to sexual intercourse is not, of itself, to be regarded as consent to the risk of consequent disease; but if V does consent to such a risk that would provide D with a defence to a charge under **s 20**.
Ireland [1998] AC 147	D made a large number of telephone calls to three women and remained silent when they answered. A psychiatrist who examined the women stated that as a result of the repeated telephone calls each of them had suffered psychological damage. D appealed against his convictions for offences contrary to **s 47** on two grounds: 1. silence cannot amount to an assault, and 2. psychological damage is not bodily harm.	1. On the *assault* issue: Where the making of a silent telephone call caused fear of immediate and unlawful violence, the caller would be guilty of an assault, if he formed *mens rea*. 2. On the meaning of *bodily* harm: In the light of contemporary knowledge covering recognisable psychiatric injuries, and bearing in mind the best current scientific appreciation of the link between the body and psychiatric injury, recognisable psychiatric illnesses fell within the phrase 'bodily harm'.

Case	Facts	Principle
Savage [1992] 1 AC 699	D threw the contents of a glass of beer over V and as she did so, the glass broke and cut V.	Her conviction for a s 20 offence was substituted with a conviction for a s 47 offence. Section 20 requires the prosecution to prove D foresaw some harm to V, but the s 47 offence does not. The prosecution must simply prove the offence of a technical assault or (as here) a battery.

🔊 Key debates

Topic	'Offences against the Person: Into the 21st Century'
Author/Academic	Michael Jefferson
Viewpoint	Offers a critique of the OAPA 1861 and includes a proposed redraft of the Act.
Source	[2012] J Crim L 472

Topic	'Sado-masochism and consent'
Author/Academic	Nicholas Bamforth
Viewpoint	Summarises the majority and dissenting opinions in *Brown* and questions whether the majority's decision to equate sado-masochism with violence *per se* is justified.
Source	[1994] Crim LR 661

Topic	'Flogging live complainants and dead horses: We may no longer need to be in bondage to *Brown*'
Author/Academic	Peter Murphy
Viewpoint	The judge in a trial dealing with the extent to which a person may consent to sado-masochistic activity provides a commentary on the law.
Source	[2011] Crim LR 758

Topic	'Criminal law and the sexual transmission of HIV: *R v Dica*'
Author/Academic	Matthew Weait
Viewpoint	This article examines the role of the criminal law in regulating the transmission of sexually transmitted diseases (STDs). Weait, widely regarded as the leading academic on this issue, reviews the previous case law and evaluates the Court of Appeal's decision in detail.
Source	(2005) 68(1) MLR 121

Problem question

Jon, who is very shy, became attracted to his next-door neighbour, Celia. Because of his shyness, he found it impossible to speak to her. Jon sometimes telephoned Celia at home and work, each time intending to express his love, but always too frightened to pluck up the courage to speak. On other occasions, Jon knocked on Celia's front door, but was too shy to wait for her to answer the door, and left.

Celia had become increasingly anxious about the silent telephone calls and anonymous knocks on her front door. Her doctor signed her off work with anxiety-related neurosis.

Aware that Celia was at home and ill, Jon persuaded his friend, Michael, to call round to Celia's house and ask if she was alright. Michael agreed. When he knocked on Celia's front door, there was no answer although he could hear music coming from the back of the house. Michael walked around to the back of the house where he saw Celia, facing the garden. Celia had not heard Michael's approach. Michael said, 'Excuse me, are you Celia?'

Celia, surprised, jumped up from her chair and spilled a cup of hot coffee down her legs, causing blistering.

Consider the criminal liability, if any, of Jon and Michael. You should not, however, consider Jon's liability, if any, as an accomplice to Michael's acts.

An outline answer is included at the end of the book.

Essay question

If individuals wish consensually to inflict harm upon one another the law should not intervene.

Discuss with reference to decided cases.

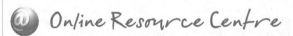

To see an outline answer to this question log on to www.oxfordtextbooks.co.uk/orc/concentrate/

#6
Sexual offences

Key facts

- Sexual offences are all governed by the **Sexual Offences Act 2003**.

- There are certain definitional elements which are common to the principal crimes. These are: V does not consent, D does not reasonably believe that V consents, and the act is sexual.

- Where the victim is aged 13 or younger, consent is irrelevant and liability as to age is strict.

- Incest is the term used to describe sexual activity between family members.

Chapter overview

Common elements studied		Offences studied and where the elements arise				
		Rape	Assault by penetration	Sexual assault	Causing sexual activity	Offences against children under 13
V does not consent	Lack of consent is conclusive	√	√	√	√	Consent is irrelevant
	Lack of consent is rebuttably presumed	√	√	√	√	Consent is irrelevant
	Definition of consent	√	√	√	√	Consent is irrelevant
D lacks a reasonable belief that V consented		√	√	√	√	Consent is irrelevant
Sexual		X	√	√	√	√
D may be male or female		X	√	√	√	√ (except for rape)
V may be male or female		√	√	√	√	√

Introduction

There are many more sexual crimes than we deal with here, but we examine those which most commonly feature (many courses do not cover these crimes and you must check on yours).

Revision tip

The **Sexual Offences Act 2003 (SOA 2003)** was a codifying Act which was the product of an independent review (Home Office, *Setting the boundaries, reforming the law on sexual offences*, Vol 1, 2000) and a White Paper (Home Office, *Protecting the Public*, Cm 5668, 2002). These are both available on the Home Office website (www.gov.uk/government/organisations/home-office). See also 'Key debates', p 80.

It is common to refer to the 'complainant' in a sexual offence rather than the 'victim', but for the sake of uniformity across the book, we will continue to use the term 'victim' or 'V'.

The common elements

The meaning of consent

The meaning of consent is key because V's lack of consent is an element of the *actus reus*, and D's belief about V's consent is an element of the *mens rea*. Consent can include various states of mind, from positive desire to reluctant acquiescence, but submission is not the same thing as consent (*Olugboja* [1982]). Although it is always a jury question, ss 74–76 SOA 2003 include a definition and some presumptions concerning this definitional element.

Revision tip

You must master the definition of consent under the **SOA 2003**. Consent in relation to sexual offences is about whether V did (and was able to) consent to the *nature and purpose* of the act, the meaning of which is explored in *Devonald* [2008] in 'Key cases', p 79.

✅ *Looking for extra marks?*

Read the revision tip above. In *R v B* [2007] it was not rape when V consented to have sexual intercourse with D, where D knew but did not disclose he was HIV positive. The Court of Appeal held that the act remained a consensual act. His failure to disclose would have been a relevant issue if he had been charged with an offence contrary to s 20 **Offences Against the Person Act 1861** (see *Dica* [2004] in 'Key cases' in chapter 5, p 66) but it was irrelevant to the question of whether V consented to the sexual activity for the purposes of proving rape.

The common elements

✳✳✳✳✳✳✳✳✳✳

There are three sections of the Act with which you must become familiar in order to understand the meaning of consent under the SOA 2003.

Section 76 provides for some *conclusive* presumptions to be made about consent:

- where D did the relevant act *and*
- intentionally deceived V as to the nature or purpose of the act or intentionally induced V to consent to the relevant act by impersonating a person known personally to V, *then*
- it is conclusively presumed that V did not consent (the *actus reus*), *and* that D did not believe that V consented (the *mens rea*).

The use of the word *purpose* in s 76 has caused academic debate (see 'Key cases', p 79 and 'Key debates', p 80).

....

Jheeta [2007] 2 Cr App R 34

D and V had met some years previously and had begun a consensual sexual relationship. V received various text messages purportedly from police officers, but in fact from D, directing her to sleep with D or she would be liable for a fine. D admitted he knew V had intercourse with him because of the texts and that she had not truly consented. D pleaded guilty to rape under the 2003 Act on the basis that his admitted behaviour fell within the ambit of s 76 of the 2003 Act. However, the Court of Appeal held that the conclusive presumption in s 76 of the 2003 Act had no application where V was deceived by D's lies. Whilst lies may be deceptive and persuasive, they would rarely go to the nature or purpose of the act, which in the case of rape was vaginal, anal, or oral intercourse. However, as D had admitted that on some occasions intercourse had taken place when V was not truly consenting, that was not a free choice or consent for the purpose of s 74 of the 2003 Act and, therefore, J's convictions for rape were safe.

....

See further 'Key debates', p 80.

Section 75 provides for some *evidential* presumptions about consent:

- where D did the relevant act, *and*
  - any person was, at the time of the relevant act or immediately before it began, using violence against V or causing V to fear that immediate violence would be used against him
  - as above but against another person
  - V was and D was not unlawfully detained at the time
  - V was asleep or otherwise unconscious at the time
  - because of V's physical disability, V would not have been able to communicate to D whether V consented
  - any person had administered to or caused to be taken by V, without V's consent, a substance which was capable of causing or enabling V to be stupefied or overpowered, *and*

- D knew that one of the circumstances listed above existed, *then*
- V is *to be taken not* to have consented *unless* sufficient evidence is adduced to raise an issue as to whether he consented, *and* D is to be taken not to have reasonably believed that V consented unless sufficient evidence is adduced to raise an issue as to whether D reasonably believed it.

Finally, s 74 provides that a person consents if he agrees by choice, and has the freedom and capacity to make that choice.

. . . .

Bree [2008] QB 131

D was charged with raping V, who was drunk at the time. The Court of Appeal held that on the proper construction of s 74, if, through drink, V had temporarily lost her capacity to choose whether to have intercourse on the relevant occasion, she was not consenting; that, however, where V had voluntarily consumed even substantial quantities of alcohol, but nevertheless remained capable of choosing whether or not to have intercourse, and in drink agreed to do so, she was consenting.

. . . .

Revision tip

The sections of the Act listed are in reverse numerical order. That is because when you are applying the law in a problem question, you might consider whether the lack of consent is conclusively presumed first. If it is, there is no need to consider the other sections. If it is not, you should state the law, rule it out quickly, and move on to s 75. Follow the same process for s 75 and finally deal with s 74. In an essay question which is more discursive and analytical, you might wish to state the definition in s 74 first, then deal with the presumptions.

✓ *Looking for extra marks?*

In *R (F) v DPP* (2013), the court held that if, before penetration, a man had made up his mind that he would penetrate and ejaculate within V's vagina contrary to her express and known consent that she would have sexual intercourse only if he wore a condom or did not ejaculate in her vagina, he had decided he would not withdraw at all, then her consent would be negated and the circumstances would fall within the statutory definition of rape. Although this was a decision of the High Court in the context of judicial review, consider the possible consequences of this decision if followed by the jury in the Crown Court. For example, if a prostitute has sexual intercourse on the basis that she or he will be paid afterwards, but the customer intends from the outset not to pay, is this rape? (*Linekar* (1995))

Belief in consent

The prosecution must prove that D did not *reasonably* believe V consented (*R v B* [2013]). Section 1(2) SOA 2003 provides that whether a belief is reasonable is to be determined having regard to all the circumstances, including any steps D has taken to ascertain whether V consented. This means that the test is *objective* to the extent that there is a reasonableness, but also *subjective* because all the circumstances includes D's personal characteristics and attributes are relevant.

In the pre-2003 Act law it was a 'defence' if D genuinely believed that V consented, even if D's belief was unreasonable. It is, in fact, wrong to say it was a defence. It is far better to say there was no offence. D's honest belief that V consented meant there was no *mens rea*; no crime. The leading case was *DPP v Morgan* [1976], which is a key case in chapter 14.

Sexual

Many crimes under the 2003 Act involve an element of 'sexual' activity, so you need to be able to define and illustrate what is and is not sexual by reference to the Act and case law. Section 78 SOA 2003 provides that an act is sexual if a reasonable person would consider that:

- whatever its circumstances or any person's purpose in relation to it, it is because of its nature sexual, or
- because of its nature it may be sexual and because of its circumstances or the purpose of any person in relation to it (or both) it is sexual.

. . . .

H [2005] 1 WLR 2005

D had attempted to pull V towards him by grabbing at a pocket on her trousers. The Court of Appeal held that the jury had to answer two questions:

1. Did they, as 12 reasonable people, consider that the touching could be sexual?
2. Did they, as 12 reasonable people, and in all the circumstances of the case, consider that the purpose of the touching had in fact been sexual? It had been open to the jury at H's trial to find the touching to have been sexual.

. . . .

Other examples include:

- touching V's breasts; *Burns* [2006]
- kissing V's face; *W* [2005]
- D rubbing his penis on V's body; *Osmani* [2006]

Rape

Rape is not an offence which was first created by the SOA 2003, but the 2003 Act did amend the existing definition to include (for the first time) transsexual defendants and oral penetration (anal rape was already part of the previous crime by the provisions of the Criminal Justice and Public Order Act 1994) (defined in Table 6.1).

Table 6.1 The definition of rape

Section 1 SOA 2003	
Actus reus	**Mens rea**
• D (who must be male) • Penetrates with his penis • The vagina, anus or mouth of V (who may be female or male) • And V does not consent	• D intends to penetrate • D does not reasonably believe that V consents

Assault by penetration

This is a completely new offence (defined in Table 6.2).

Table 6.2 The definition of assault by penetration

Section 2 SOA 2003	
Actus reus	**Mens rea**
• D (who may be male or female) • Penetrates • The vagina or anus of V (who may be female or male) • With a part of his/her body or anything else • Sexually • And V does not consent	• D intends to penetrate • D does not reasonably believe that V consents

Sexual assault

This offence replaces the old crimes of indecent assault (defined in Table 6.3).

Table 6.3 The definition of sexual assault

Section 3 SOA 2003	
Actus reus	**Mens rea**
• D (who may be male or female) • Touches • V (who may be female or male) • Sexually • And V does not consent	• D intends to touch • D does not reasonably believe that V consents

Causing sexual activity

This is also a new offence (defined in Table 6.4).

Table 6.4 The definition of causing sexual activity

Section 4 SOA 2003	
Actus reus	*Mens rea*
<ul><li>D (who may be male or female)</li><li>Causes</li><li>V (who may be female or male)</li><li>To engage in an activity which is sexual</li><li>And V does not consent</li></ul>	<ul><li>D intends to cause V to engage in an activity which is sexual</li><li>D does not reasonably believe that V consents</li></ul>

Rape of a child under 13

Note that for this offence, consent is neither an element of the *actus reus* nor an element of the *mens rea*. See *R v G* [2009]. The offence is defined in Table 6.5.

Table 6.5 The definition of rape of a child under 13

Section 5 SOA 2003	
Actus reus	*Mens rea*
<ul><li>D (who must be male)</li><li>Penetrates with his penis</li><li>The vagina, anus or mouth of V (who may be female or male)</li><li>And V is under the age of 13</li></ul>	<ul><li>D intends to penetrate</li></ul>

Assault by penetration of a child under 13

Consent is also irrelevant for this offence, which is defined in Table 6.6.

Table 6.6 The definition of assault by penetration of a child under 13

Section 6 SOA 2003	
Actus reus	*Mens rea*
<ul><li>D (who may be male or female)</li><li>Penetrates</li><li>The vagina or anus of V</li><li>With a part of his/her body or anything else</li><li>Sexually</li><li>And V is under the age of 13</li></ul>	<ul><li>D intends to penetrate</li></ul>

Sexual assault of a child under 13

Consent is also irrelevant for this offence, which is defined in Table 6.7.

Table 6.7 The definition of sexual assault of a child under 13

Section 7 SOA 2003	
Actus reus	***Mens rea***
• D (who may be male or female) • Touches • V (who may be female or male) • Sexually • And V is under the age of 13	• D intends to touch

Sexual activity with a child over 13

This offence is strict liability in respect of *consent* (or lack of) but not in respect of V's *age*. The offence is defined in Table 6.8.

Table 6.8 The definition of sexual activity with a child over 13

Section 9 SOA 2003	
Actus reus	***Mens rea***
• D (who may be male or female) is aged 18 or older • Touches • V (who may be female or male) • Sexually • And V is aged 15 or younger	• D intends to touch • D lacks reasonable belief that V is 16 or over

Incest

Incest is the term used to describe sexual activity between family members.

Sexual activity with a child family member

Consent is irrelevant for this offence, which is defined in Table 6.9.

Table 6.9 The definition of sexual activity with a child family member

Section 25 SOA 2003	
Actus reus	*Mens rea*
• D (who may be male or female) • Touches • V (who may be female or male) • Sexually • D is related to V • And V is under the age of 18	• D intends to touch • D is reasonably expected to know V is a relation • D lacks reasonable belief that V is 18 or over

Family relations are defined (s 27) as:

- parent
- grandparent
- brother or sister
- half-brother or half-sister
- aunt or uncle
- foster parent (past or present).

Sex by penetration of an adult relative

This offence is defined in Table 6.10.

Table 6.10 The definition of sex by penetration of an adult relative

Section 64 SOA 2003	
Actus reus	*Mens rea*
• D (who may be male or female) is aged 16 or older • Penetrates V's vagina or anus with any body part or object OR V's mouth with his penis • Sexually • V is aged 18 or older • And D is related to V	• D intends to penetrate • D is reasonably expected to know V is a relation

The offence under s 64 is mirrored by an offence under s 65 by the V who has allowed the penetration in the s 64 offence. V becomes D, and D (s 64) we shall call 'R', for relative. The s 65 offence is defined in Table 6.11.

Table 6.11 The definition of sex by penetration of an adult relative; consenting to penetration

Section 65 SOA 2003	
Actus reus	**Mens rea**
• R (who may be male or female) is aged 18 or older • Penetrates D's vagina or anus with any body part or object OR D's mouth with his penis • Sexually • D consents to penetration • And R is related to D	• D is reasonably expected to know R is a relation

 **(✱) Key cases**

Case	Facts	Principle
Bree [2008] QB 131	The defendant was charged with raping V who was drunk at the time.	The Court of Appeal held that on the proper construction of **s 74**, if, through drink, V had temporarily lost her capacity to choose whether to have intercourse on the relevant occasion, she was not consenting; that, however, where V had voluntarily consumed even substantial quantities of alcohol, but nevertheless remained capable of choosing whether or not to have intercourse, and in drink agreed to do so, she was consenting.
Devonald [2008] EWCA Crim 527	V was a 16-year-old boy and D was the father of V's ex-girlfriend. D sought to humiliate V, thinking V had treated his daughter badly, by corresponding with V over the internet apparently impersonating a young woman. D persuaded V to masturbate in front of a webcam. The issue was whether V had consented to engage in masturbation.	It was open to the jury to conclude that V had been deceived as to the *purpose* of the masturbation. Whilst the *nature* of the act was undoubtedly sexual, its *purpose* encompassed rather more than the specific purpose of sexual gratification.
Jheeta [2007] 2 Cr App R 34	D persuaded V that she was being stalked, but in fact he was the stalker. D lied in order for V to have sexual intercourse with him. For a fuller summary of the facts, see p 72, *Jheeta*.	D had committed rape. Although his lies did not conclusively prove the lack of consent (**s 76**), D's admission that he knew V had not truly consented showed V had not made a free choice for the purpose of **s 74** of the **SOA 2003**.

Key debates

✳✳✳✳✳✳✳✳✳✳

Topic	'The Sexual Offences Act 2003: (1) Rape, sexual assaults and the problems of consent'
Author/ Academic	Jennifer Temkin and Andrew Ashworth
Viewpoint	This article explores the main offences considered here and assesses whether the then new **Sexual Offences Act 2003** meets its aims. Although a little dated now, the article is very useful as a summary of the crimes and also provides a critique of the law governing consent under the **SOA** (both as *actus reus* and *mens rea*).
Source	[2004] Crim LR 328

Topic	'The meaning of consent within the Sexual Offences Act 2003'
Author/ Academic	David Selfe
Viewpoint	The article queries whether **s 76 SOA 2003** is a consolidation of the common law 'nature and quality' test, or whether the word 'purpose' is capable of carrying a broader interpretation.
Source	[2008] 178 Crim Law 3–5

Topic	'The concept of consent under the Sexual Offences Act 2003'
Author/ Academic	Jesse Elvin
Viewpoint	The article examines the correct interpretation of **ss 74–76** of the **SOA 2003** and argues that the Act does not provide a clear general definition of consent.
Source	(2008) 72(6) J Crim L 519–36

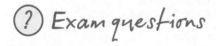

Problem question

Andrew is a dentist with a number of female patients. Whilst treating Barbara, he told her she was very pretty and stroked her hair. Barbara was very uncomfortable with Andrew's acts but was too shy to ask him to stop.

Another patient, Cindy, needed to be given a mild anaesthetic for Andrew to carry out a minor operation. Cindy remained conscious but felt dizzy, sick, and disorientated under the influence of the anaesthetic. Cindy told Andrew she felt 'very funny'. Andrew completed the procedure and then asked Cindy if she would have sexual intercourse with him. Cindy reluctantly agreed, but that evening, after the effects of the anaesthetic had worn off, Cindy went to the police and told them Andrew had raped her.

Discuss Andrew's criminal liability, if any, for offences under the **Sexual Offences Act 2003**.

An outline answer is included at the end of the book.

Essay question

The offences under the **Sexual Offences Act 2003** are unique regarding the *mens rea* for a serious crime because they are phrased in terms of reasonableness of belief, not simply honest belief.

Consider the truth of this assertion.

To see an outline answer to this question log on to www.oxfordtextbooks.co.uk/orc/concentrate/

#7
Homicide I

Key facts

- The most serious crime in English law is **murder**.

- Murder is where D kills V and D intends to kill or intends to cause GBH.

- The most common criticism of the offence of murder is that the sentence is mandatory irrespective of whether the *mens rea* is the more serious form (intent to kill) or the less serious form (intent to cause GBH).

- There are three partial defences to murder; diminished responsibility under the Homicide Act 1957 as amended, loss of control under the Coroners and Justice Act 2009, and suicide pact. We will consider the first two.

- These are *partial* defences because they result in a conviction for manslaughter rather than a full acquittal.

Chapter overview

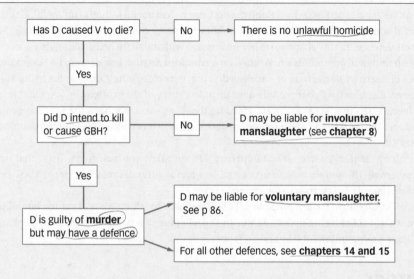

Has D caused V to die? — No → There is no unlawful homicide

Yes

Did D intend to kill or cause GBH? — No → D may be liable for **involuntary manslaughter** (see **chapter 8**)

Yes

D is guilty of **murder** but may have a defence → D may be liable for **voluntary manslaughter**. See p 86.

→ For all other defences, see **chapters 14 and 15**

Introduction

Not all **homicides** *are unlawful.* The word homicide simply means the act of a human being killing another human being (Oxford English Dictionary), and not all killing is unlawful. Examples of lawful homicides include where a soldier kills an enemy combatant in war, or where D kills V in self-defence. In this chapter, we are concerned with unlawful homicides only.

Not all unlawful homicides are studied on a standard English law degree. For example, the crimes of death by dangerous or careless driving, genocide, infanticide, or assisting suicide are rarely examined. If your module does include a study of these offences, you must refer to your lecture/seminar notes and a standard textbook, as we do not have the space to consider them here. We outline the main issues concerning the offence of corporate manslaughter in chapter 10.

Not all life sentences are served in prison. Do not allow yourself to be distracted by the (controversial) life sentence for murder and/or when an offender may be released on licence. Criminal liability is our focus and sentence is not.

Not all manslaughters are the same. This is an issue to which we will return later, but be aware we are considering manslaughter in this chapter as a partial *defence* to murder, and in chapter 8 as an unlawful homicide *offence.*

Murder

Murder is a common law offence. Even though there is a **Homicide Act** (of 1957) which we will soon consider, it does not define murder.

Actus reus

All unlawful homicides have the same *actus reus*. Defined in the seventeenth century by Sir Edward Coke, it is where D 'unlawfully killeth ... any reasonable creature *in rerum natura* under the [Queen's] peace'. In modern language, this is simplified as:

* D causes V, a human being, to die

* during peacetime.

The most commonly examined element of the *actus reus* is causation which was considered in chapter 2 and which is not repeated here.

Mens rea

The *mens rea* of murder is malice aforethought which is found in the traditional definition by Coke and is mentioned in **s 1 Homicide Act 1957** (although not as part of the definition of the crime, because the crime is a common law offence). However, the *mens rea* may also be described as intention to kill or cause GBH, as stated in numerous cases, but most notably *Moloney* [1985].

Revision tip

Why not put them together?

> The *mens rea* for murder is malice aforethought (Coke) which is satisfied on proof of intention to kill or cause GBH (*Moloney* [1985], HL).

> You must, however, appreciate that there are more marks available for applying the law to the question (either a problem question or an essay) than in simply stating an accurate definition.

What is more important to be able to discuss is the fact that the *mens rea* for murder encompasses **implied malice**. That is the term we give to the 'lesser' *mens rea*: intention to cause GBH. As we have seen in chapter 5, really serious harm, or just serious harm, amounts to GBH and because GBH does not have to be life-threatening, this means that where D intends to cause GBH, but V dies, D can be convicted of murder even though death was not foreseen.

....

Cunningham (Anthony Barry) [1982] AC 566

> D, in a jealous rage and a wholly unprovoked attack, killed V. The prosecution conceded that D did not intend to kill V, but the jury found he intended to cause V serious harm. The House of Lords approved its own previous decision in *Hyam* [1975] that implied malice is sufficient *mens rea* for murder.

....

✅ *Looking for extra marks?*

The minority opinions of Lords Diplock and Kilbrandon in *Hyam* [1975] contain criticisms of implied malice. Your understanding of this may be useful in an essay question on the definition and scope of murder, and also in a problem question where D intends to cause serious injury but does not intend or even foresee death.

Examination questions often require you to consider the distinction between direct and oblique intention (perhaps more importantly, between recklessness and oblique intention). The authority is *Woollin* [1999] which you will find in chapter 3 in Table 3.2, Table 3.3, and in 'Key cases' in chapter 3, p 39.

Revision tip

Refer back to chapter 3, 'Intention', p 32 and 'Recklessness', p 34. Note that you are considering two issues: (1) If the result was not D's desire, how much foresight is needed for the jury to find D had intention (ie where is the line between recklessness and intention), and (2) if D did foresee the result as a virtual certainty, does that *allow* the jury to find intention, or *oblige* them to do so? See further *Stringer* [2008].

Voluntary manslaughter

The word **manslaughter** has a great deal of work to do in the criminal law. Generally regarded as a lesser homicide than murder, there are two types of manslaughter, voluntary and involuntary, terms which tend to confuse rather than clarify.

The two words (voluntary and involuntary) also have a lot of work to do in the criminal law, and context means everything. We have already seen that an *actus reus* committed involuntarily gives rise to the 'defence' of automatism. Later, we will see that intoxication by drink or drugs is either voluntary or involuntary. In this context, however, 'voluntary' before 'manslaughter' simply means the prosecution can prove D formed the *mens rea* for murder, but D is convicted of **voluntary manslaughter** because he falls within one of the three partial defences.

In light of the mandatory sentence for murder, these partial defences are very important. They take D outside the mandatory sentence, but do not result in an acquittal. The maximum sentence for voluntary manslaughter is a discretionary life sentence.

The scope of the partial defences has recently been amended by the **Coroners and Justice Act 2009** (C&JA 2009). The relevant provisions came into force in October 2010. In a nutshell, the defences of diminished responsibility and provocation have been changed as shown in Table 7.1.

Table 7.1 Voluntary manslaughter: the main changes in the 2009 Act

Partial defence	Old source of law	New source of law	Main change
Diminished responsibility	**Section 2** of the **Homicide Act 1957 (HA 1957)**	An amended **s 2** of the **HA 1957**	The terms and definitions have changed. Some case law might remain relevant
Provocation	Common law and **s 3** of the **HA 1957**	A new defence of loss of self-control; **ss 54 and 55** of the **C&JA 2009**.	Although provocation has been abolished, some of the old case law remains relevant because the new defence is designed to replicate *some* of the old law (but not all)

Diminished responsibility

Section 2 HA 1957 as amended by **s 52** of the **C&JA 2009** provides:

(1) A person ('D') who kills or is a party to the killing of another is not to be convicted of murder if D was suffering from an abnormality of mental functioning which—

  (a) arose from a recognised medical condition,

(b) substantially impaired D's ability to do one or more of the things mentioned in subsection (1A), and

(c) provides an explanation for D's acts and omissions in doing or being a party to the killing.

(1A) Those things are—

(a) to understand the nature of D's conduct;

(b) to form a rational judgment;

(c) to exercise self-control.

(1B) For the purposes of subsection (1)(c), an abnormality of mental functioning provides an explanation for D's conduct if it causes, or is a significant contributory factor in causing, D to carry out that conduct.

(2) On a charge of murder, it shall be for the defence to prove that the person charged is by virtue of this section not liable to be convicted of murder.

There are *four* elements to the defence under the amended s 2(1):

- Abnormality of mental functioning
- which arises from a recognised medical condition, and
- caused or was a significant contributory factor in causing D to act as he did (in killing), and
- the abnormality substantially impaired D's ability.

Revision tip

When law is amended/repealed, it is common for students to face a 'compare and contrast the old with the new' in the exam. You need to be able to explain the main changes and to comment on whether the changes were either necessary or beneficial to the stated aim of the change. We highlight the significant changes later in this chapter, but you are strongly advised to read the articles in this chapter's 'Key debates' too.

Abnormality of mental functioning

Under the **HA 1957** as originally enacted, the first element of the defence was abnormality of *mind*. The authority on the meaning of *mind* was the case of *Byrne* [1960]. The definition was very wide and most abnormal states of mind, from quite minor to very serious, could fall within it.

. . . .

Byrne [1960] 2 QB 396

D was charged with the murder of a young girl whom he had strangled and whose dead body he had mutilated. D suffered from abnormal sexual urges which were so strong D could not resist them. The Court of Appeal defined abnormality of mind as a state of mind so different from that of ordinary human beings that the reasonable man would term it abnormal. It is wide enough to cover the mind's activities in all its aspects, not only the perception of physical acts and matters, and the ability to form a rational judgement as to whether an act is right or wrong, but also the ability to exercise will power to control physical acts in accordance with that rational judgement.

We have recited this in full, because there are elements of that judgment that appear in the amended s 2 HA 1957 (see s 2(1A) in particular), but also to draw your attention to the change in terminology: *mind* has become *mental functioning*, but the latter is not defined in the amended defence and there is no reason to suppose it is, *per se*, any narrower.

Revision tip

Be aware of the distinction between abnormality of mental functioning for diminished responsibility (a partial defence to murder) and disease of mind for insanity (a general defence, available to any crime). As you will see in chapter 14, disease of mind is much narrower than abnormality of mental functioning and, if D pleads diminished responsibility on a murder charge, there is nothing preventing the prosecution proving insanity to counter it (refer to s 6 **Criminal Procedure (Insanity) Act 1964**).

Recognised medical condition

Under the original s 2 HA 1957, the abnormality must have arisen from 'a condition of arrested or retarded development of mind or any inherent causes or induced by disease or injury'. Although this exhaustive list had the potential severely to restrict the availability of the defence, the terms used were wide enough to include most states of mind. In particular, 'any inherent cause' included:

- Depression (*Ahluwahlia* [1992])
- Battered women syndrome (*Hobson* [1998])
- Mental illness (*Sanderson* (1994)).

The new cause is more simply a 'recognised medical condition' which includes psychiatric, psychological, and physical conditions. It may include medical conditions associated with alcoholism, but it does not include voluntary acute intoxication, whether from alcohol or other substance (*Dowds* [2012]). The new term is potentially wider than the previous term; but the next two elements considered might restrict the scope of the reformulated defence.

Substantial impairment of D's ability

Whether D's ability was substantially impaired at the time of the killing is a question of fact for the jury.

Revision tip

When you are answering problem questions in the exam, do try to apply the law to the facts and don't simply conclude it is all 'for the jury to decide'. *You are the judge and you are the jury,* so you must be prepared to try to reach conclusions on the facts of the question (based of course on legal authority).

The word 'substantial' was also used in the original s 2, and the meaning of it is still the same ('less than total and more than trivial', *Lloyd* [1967], for the jury to decide, using their common sense, *Baker* [2012]). The substantial impairment has to be of D's ability to:

* understand the nature of his conduct,
* form a rational judgement, or
* exercise self-control.

Although these elements echo the terms used in *Byrne*, and are therefore wide in scope, they are narrower than the previous requirement (D's general responsibility for his acts/omissions); and they probably exclude a defendant who commits a 'mercy killing' knowing what he is doing.

✔ *Looking for extra marks?*

Using a standard criminal law textbook, review some of the cases decided under the original s 2 and hypothesise whether the defendant would have a substantial impairment of his ability under the reformulated defence.

Provides an explanation for D's acts, etc

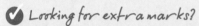

This installs a causal connection between the abnormality and the killing. The requirement makes explicit what was implicit in the previous s 2 and through case law.

....

Dietschmann [2003] 1 AC 1209

D killed a man whilst under the influence of alcohol. D believed V had insulted D's aunt, to whom D had been very close. At trial, psychiatrists for both parties agreed that D was suffering from an abnormality of mind which manifested itself as a delayed grief reaction, or adjustment disorder, following the death of his aunt. The House of Lords held that the defence of diminished responsibility did not require D to prove that had he not consumed alcohol he would still have killed. The question for the jury was whether *the underlying condition* (the grief disorder) substantially impaired D's responsibility for the killing.

....

We would now ask whether the recognised medical condition (here that is the grief disorder and not the alcohol) caused an abnormality of mental functioning, which substantially impaired D's ability to form rational judgement or exercise self-control, and whether the abnormality was a significant factor causing D to act as he did. This is a change in form, but probably not in substance.

The burden of proof

The burden of proving diminished responsibility lies on D. The standard of proof is on a balance of probabilities. Section 2(2) has not been amended by the C&JA 2009.

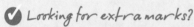 Looking for extra marks?

Why doesn't the allocation of the burden of proof to D violate Article 6(2) European Convention on Human Rights? See *Lambert; Ali; Jordan* [2002].

Loss of control

This is a new partial defence; it replaces that of provocation under common law and s 3 of the HA 1957, which provided a defence where

- there were things said or done,
- D actually lost self-control, and
- the reasonable man would have done what D did.

Section 56 C&JA 2009 repealed s 3 of the HA 1957 and ss 54 and 55 replaced provocation with a new partial defence, also based on loss of self-control. Section 54 provides:

(1) Where a person ('D') kills or is a party to the killing of another ('V'), D is not to be convicted of murder [but of manslaughter] if—

    (a) D's acts and omissions in doing or being a party to the killing resulted from D's loss of self-control,

    (b) the loss of self-control had a qualifying trigger, and

    (c) a person of D's sex and age, with a normal degree of tolerance and self-restraint and in the circumstances of D, might have reacted in the same or in a similar way to D.

(2) For the purposes of subsection (1)(a), it does not matter whether or not the loss of control was sudden.

(3) In subsection (1)(c) the reference to 'the circumstances of D' is a reference to all of D's circumstances other than those whose only relevance to D's conduct is that they bear on D's general capacity for tolerance or self-restraint.

There are *three* elements to the defence:

- D lost self-control
- the loss of control had a qualifying trigger (s 55) and
- an objective test.

There are **two** qualifying triggers (either or both may be satisfied):

- where D's loss of self-control was attributable to D's fear of serious violence from V against D or another identified person (s 55(3)), and/or
- D's loss of self-control was attributable to a thing or things done or said (or both) which constituted circumstances of an extremely grave character, *and* caused D to have a justifiable sense of being seriously wronged (s 55(4)).

Loss of self-control

Under s 54, D must have lost self-control, but under s 54(2), the loss of self-control need not have been sudden. This provision reverses the common law. *Duffy* [1949] provided that D had to have 'a sudden and temporary loss of self-control, rendering the accused so subject to passion as to make him or her for the moment not master of his mind'. One of the effects of the law was therefore to exclude non-sudden (or non-immediate) losses of self-control from the scope of the defence and this had an effect on battered women who kill.

·····

Ahluwalia [1992] 4 All ER 889

D had suffered violence and abuse from her husband over a long period. After one evening during which she had been threatened, D went to bed, but thinking about her husband's behaviour was unable to sleep. She went downstairs, poured petrol into a bucket, lit a candle, then returned and set fire to her husband's bedroom. He died from his injuries. The jury convicted her of murder. The defence appeal centred on the meaning of loss of self-control under *Duffy* [1949] because, particularly in the case of abused wives, the act could be the result of a 'slowburn' reaction rather than an immediate loss of self-control. Their Lordships, however, held *Duffy* to be good law; they allowed her appeal in respect of diminished responsibility.

·····

The Law Commission, whose recommendations led to the C&JA 2009, had proposed that the 'loss of self-control' requirement be abolished but, as you can see, it is still a requirement and leaves us with an odd situation: the term 'loss of self-control' implies an impulsive reaction which occurs quickly; how could such a reaction ever be not sudden? There is a second issue, too, which is s 54(4), which provides the defence fails if D acted with a 'considered desire for revenge'; surely there can be no actual loss of self-control anyway if there is a 'considered' desire for anything. Section 54(4) seems, at best, superfluous. (See further 'Key debates', p 95.)

The qualifying triggers

The two qualifying triggers can be categorised as the 'fear' trigger (of serious violence from V against D or another identified person) and the 'anger' trigger (a thing or things done or said (or both) which constituted circumstances of an extremely grave character, and caused D to have a justifiable sense of being seriously wronged).

The fear trigger is clearly aimed at the battered spouse cases where D cannot plead self-defence or duress (because of the lack of imminence in the potential attack from the spouse and/or because of the amount of force used; see chapter 15). The anger trigger is a parallel to the previous defence of provocation, but note the severity of the language used ('extremely grave' … 'justifiable' … 'seriously'), terms which limit the defence's application. For an illustration of the thresholds imposed by this language, see *Dawes* [2013], per Lord Judge CJ.

There are certain statutory exclusions from the qualifying trigger: s 55(6) provides that D's fear or sense of being seriously wronged must be disregarded if D incited it as an excuse to use violence. Further, although the sexual infidelity of another is *not* a qualifying trigger (s 55(6)(c)), in *R v Clinton* [2012], the Court of Appeal held that the jury *may* take sexual infidelity into account when determining the accused's 'circumstances' for the purposes of s 54(1)(c) of the Act, and further that 'where sexual infidelity is integral to and forms an essential part of the context in which to make a just evaluation whether *a qualifying trigger* properly falls within the ambit of subsections 55(3) and (4), the prohibition in section 55(6)(c) does *not operate to exclude it'* (emphasis added).

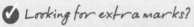 **Looking for extra marks?**

Can you imagine a couple of scenarios in preparation for the exam? One should be where the sole cause of the loss of self-control was V's sexual infidelity (so would have to be excluded), and another where (on more complex facts) V's sexual infidelity is part of a wider context and therefore could be relevant to the qualifying trigger (probably using the 'anger' trigger).

The objective test

Under the common law and s 3 HA 1957, D was compared to the reasonable man for the jury to have an objective standard against which D's actions and reactions could be assessed. The question, however, was how much the reasonable person resembled the defendant; to answer this question, the law distinguished those characteristics:

- which affected the gravity of the provocation (how serious was the provocation *to D*), from
- those which were peculiar to D's *level of self-control* (given the level of provocation, did D show a reasonable level of self-control?).

Basically, if the provocative conduct was directed at a characteristic of the defendant, that was a characteristic which affected the gravity of the provocation and that characteristic was relevant to the reasonable man.

Morhall [1996] AC 90

D, a glue-sniffing addict, was taunted by V about his addiction. The House of Lords held that D's addiction to glue sniffing was a characteristic of particular relevance to the provocation on the facts. The jury's task was to consider the effect of the provoking words on a person with the ordinary amount of self-control who had the defendant's characteristics, history, and circumstances in so far as the jury thought those would affect the gravity of the provocation.

D's age and sex were also relevant to the gravity of the provocation.

Camplin [1978] AC 705

D, aged 15, killed V by splitting his skull with a chapatti pan. At D's trial for murder, D claimed provocation on the ground that V had raped and then laughed at him. The House of Lords held that the jury should take into consideration those factors, including D's age and physical characteristics, which in their opinion would have affected the gravity of the provocation.

However, if D had a lower than normal level of self-control, that did not *per se* affect the gravity of the provocation.

Smith (Morgan) [2001] AC 146

D had an argument with V about the alleged theft by V of some of D's tools. D had clinical depression and brain damage, which caused D to be abnormally disinhibited, and lose his self-control more readily than an ordinary person. Notwithstanding the existence of diminished responsibility as a suitable defence in such circumstances, Lord Hoffmann, delivering the speech of a bare majority in the House of Lords, held the question for the jury on the objective test was whether they thought 'the behaviour of the accused had measured up to the standard of self-control which ought reasonably to have been expected of him', although it was still necessary for the jury 'to apply an objective standard of behaviour which society was entitled to expect'.

Smith (Morgan) was doubted (some say that notwithstanding it was a House of Lords' decision, it was actually overruled) by the Privy Council's decision in *AG for Jersey v Holley*.

Attorney-General for Jersey v Holley [2005] 2 AC 580

D, who was a chronic alcoholic, killed his girlfriend in a quarrel while under the influence of drink. D adduced expert medical evidence to the effect that his alcoholism was a disease and, in consequence, a characteristic of which the jury should take account when assessing his loss of self-control. The Privy Council held that the jury should be directed to assess D's loss of self-control by applying a uniform, objective standard of the degree of self-control to be expected of an ordinary person of the defendant's age and sex with ordinary powers of self-control. It was not open to courts to develop a more flexible standard which permitted a jury to take account of the defendant's particular abnormalities.

Under s 54 C&JA 2009 there is still an objective test. The reasonable person is replaced with the ordinary person. There is explicit reference to a person of D's age and sex (reflecting the law from *Camplin*), with a normal degree of tolerance and self-restraint (codifying the *Holley* test). However, instead of 'characteristics', the new defence requires the jury to examine the 'circumstances' of D. It is far from clear, therefore, whether this permits facts such as *Morhall* to be covered in the new defence. Certainly, the voluntary consumption of alcohol is not, both for consistency across the criminal law and for public policy, *Asmelash* [2013].

✅ *Looking for extra marks?*

Do you agree that age and sex should be taken into consideration when assessing loss of self-control? Why?

The burden of proof

The burden of proof in relation to loss of self-control lies on the prosecution. This means that where there is sufficient evidence of the defence (raised by D or another witness), the prosecution must disprove it beyond reasonable doubt. 'Sufficient' here means that, in the opinion of the trial judge, a jury, properly directed, could reasonably conclude that the defence might apply.

 ✱ *Key cases*

Case	Facts	Principle
Attorney-General for Jersey v Holley [2005] 2 AC 580	D, who was a chronic alcoholic, killed his girlfriend in a quarrel while under the influence of drink. D adduced expert medical evidence to the effect that his alcoholism was a disease, and in consequence a characteristic of which the jury should take account when assessing his loss of self-control.	The Privy Council held that the jury should be directed to assess D's loss of self-control by applying a uniform, objective standard of the degree of self-control to be expected of an ordinary person of the defendant's age and sex with ordinary powers of self-control. It was not open to courts to develop a more flexible standard which permitted a jury to take account of the defendant's particular abnormalities.

Case	Facts	Principle
Byrne [1960] 2 QB 396	D was charged with the murder of a young girl whom he had strangled and whose dead body he had mutilated. There was evidence that D suffered from abnormal sexual urges which were so strong D could not resist them.	The Court of Appeal defined abnormality of mind as a state of mind so different from that of ordinary human beings that the reasonable man would term it abnormal. It is wide enough to cover the mind's activities in all its aspects, not only the perception of physical acts and matters, and the ability to form a rational judgement as to whether an act is right or wrong, but also the ability to exercise will power to control physical acts in accordance with that rational judgement.
Camplin [1978] AC 705	D, aged 15, killed V by splitting his skull with a chapatti pan. At D's trial for murder, D claimed provocation on the ground that V had raped him and then laughed at him.	The jury should take into consideration those factors, including D's age and physical characteristics, which in their opinion would have affected the gravity of the provocation.

⟨⟩ Key debates

Topic	'The Coroners and Justice Act 2009: a "dog's breakfast" of homicide reform'
Author/Academic	Jo Miles
Viewpoint	This is a critical and evaluative article on the background to the changes, the Parliamentary process behind the enactment of the Bill, the operation of the defences, and whether the sections as enacted meet the purpose(s) for which they were enacted.
Source	[2009] 10 Arch News 6

Topic	'The Coroners and Justice Act 2009—partial defences to murder (1) Loss of Control'
Author/Academic	Alan Norrie
Viewpoint	The author gives a detailed analysis of the scope of the new loss of self-control defence and, where relevant, compares the new defence to the repealed defence of provocation.
Source	[2010] Crim LR 275

Exam questions

✳✳✳✳✳✳✳✳✳✳

Topic	'The Coroners and Justice Act 2009—partial defences to murder (2) The new diminished responsibility plea'
Author/Academic	JD Mackay
Viewpoint	The author gives a detailed analysis of the scope of the reformulated defence and, where relevant, compares the availability of the defence to the old **s 2** defence. He questions whether the reformulation meets the stated aims of the change.
Source	[2010] Crim LR 290

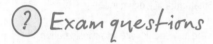

(?) Exam questions

Problem question

Kathy is a radical who is opposed to a government plan to build a nuclear power station near her home. The proposal is supported by her local MP, Lenny. One evening, Lenny hosts a public meeting at a local school.

Kathy plants a bomb at the school, but telephones and leaves a message that the bomb will explode at 8 pm and the school should be evacuated. The bomb explosion is designed to raise awareness of the unpopularity of the proposal to build the nuclear power station among the local population.

Due to a problem with the school's telephone answering machine, the message is not heard. The meeting starts at 7.30 pm and there are over 200 people in attendance. The bomb explodes at 7.35 pm due to faulty wiring. Forty people are killed in the blast.

Discuss Kathy's liability, if any, for murder.

An outline answer is included at the end of the book.

Essay question

> The abolition of the partial defence of provocation should enable battered women who kill to be convicted of manslaughter rather than murder.

Discuss the statement above with reference to **ss 54 and 55** of the **Coroners and Justice Act 2009**.

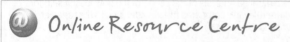

@ Online Resource Centre

To see an outline answer to this question log on to www.oxfordtextbooks.co.uk/orc/concentrate/

#8
Homicide II

Key facts

- An unlawful homicide committed without the *mens rea* for murder is involuntary manslaughter.
- There are three classes of **involuntary manslaughter**:
  - reckless manslaughter,
  - unlawful act manslaughter, and
  - gross negligence manslaughter.

Chapter overview

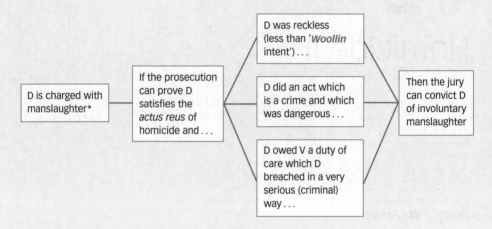

* It is possible that D is charged with murder, and manslaughter is an alternative count on the indictment.

Introduction

Many criminal law academics are of the view that there are two classes of involuntary manslaughter, and certainly you will see that the focus of this chapter is on two classes, but we must also recognise the view (of the Law Commission among others) that there is a type of unlawful killing which is not murder, but nor is it unlawful act or gross negligence manslaughter. Reckless manslaughter might be thought of as 'not-murder manslaughter', an unusual term which is explored in the next section.

Reckless manslaughter

Actus reus

Let us clear the simplest issue out of the way immediately; the prosecution must prove D caused V to die (see chapters 2 and 7 for the *actus reus* of homicide). We acknowledge that factually and legally causation is anything but simple, but in this context the more complex issue is what the definitional elements of this offence are.

Not-murder manslaughter?

If we move on to consideration of *mens rea*, what is the *mens rea* of reckless manslaughter? If, following *Woollin* [1999], a jury finds that D did foresee GBH as a probability, but did not foresee it as a virtual certainty, what is the outcome? It is not murder, so can it be manslaughter on the basis of D's foresight of harm or worse to V? The little-reported case of *Lidar* (1999) supports the conclusion that there is a reckless, less-than-oblique intent, form of unlawful homicide.

....

Lidar (1999) 4 Archbold News 3

D drove away from a fight with one of the antagonists, V, hanging from the passenger window of his car, still fighting with one of D's passengers inside. D accelerated and V fell under the wheels of D's car. D was convicted of reckless manslaughter and the Court of Appeal upheld his conviction. The prosecution has to prove an obvious risk of serious harm from D's conduct and either D's indifference to that risk, or foresight of it with a determination nevertheless to run it.

....

So *what* has to be foreseen? In *Stone and Dobinson* [1977], which you will find in 'Key cases', p 108, the Court of Appeal held that D has to disregard recklessly a risk to V's health and welfare or actually foresee the risk, but *Lidar* above suggests that D has to foresee at least serious harm.

Unlawful act manslaughter

The authority on this class of manslaughter is *DPP v Newbury and Jones* [1977] which you will find in 'Key cases', p 108. This offence is called either constructive or unlawful act manslaughter, and the terms are interchangeable. It is called constructive manslaughter because liability for manslaughter is built up from a baseline of another crime. In this respect, it operates similarly to s 47 OAPA. Liability has been built (*constructed*) from a lesser crime into a much more serious crime; hence *constructive* manslaughter.

As the offence requires a 'base' crime on which to build liability, the prosecution must therefore prove there is a crime (*an unlawful act*) first, and then that death was caused; hence *unlawful act* manslaughter. What the title unlawful act omits, however, is that the act must also be dangerous. Figure 8.1 presents the argument in diagrammatic form.

Figure 8.1 Unlawful act manslaughter

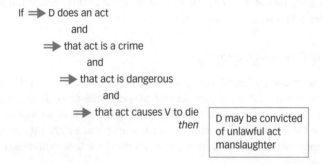

If ⟹ D does an act
and
⟹ that act is a crime
and
⟹ that act is dangerous
and
⟹ that act causes V to die
then | D may be convicted of unlawful act manslaughter

Revision tip

Once you have learnt the four-stage test set out in Figure 8.1, and understood it, illustrate each stage with cases, and make sure you are able to apply the law accurately to the question.

The definitional elements of unlawful act manslaughter

D does an act

There must be an act and that act must be intentional (ie deliberate rather than, say, negligent). Where death is caused by an omission and the prosecution cannot prove murder, the only forms of manslaughter available are the reckless or gross negligence forms (*Lowe* [1973]).

The act must be unlawful

First, an act which is lawful *per se* cannot be used as the basis for unlawful act manslaughter simply by reason of the manner in which it was carried out. For example, driving is lawful *per se*, so there can be no unlawful act manslaughter by careless driving which causes death (*Andrews v DPP* [1937]). Secondly, the prosecution must prove a *complete* base crime has been committed, and that means both the *actus reus* and *mens rea* of the base crime.

Lamb [1967] 2 QB 981

D, in jest, pointed a revolver at V, who joined in the game. The revolver had five chambers, in two of which were live bullets, neither of which was in the chamber opposite the barrel when D pulled the trigger. The chamber rotated before firing, a bullet was struck by the striking pin and V, D's friend, was killed. The Court of Appeal held that as the prosecution had been unable to prove D had the *mens rea* for assault (intention or recklessness to cause V to apprehend immediate unlawful harm) there was no complete base crime and therefore no manslaughter.

There is no restriction on the *type* of crime which can be relied on for an unlawful act manslaughter base crime, and it does not have to be aimed at another person, *Goodfellow* (1986)—provided it is dangerous (see 'The act must be dangerous', p 101).

✔ *Looking for extra marks?*

In *Andrews* [2002] the base crime was one of strict liability. In *Lamb* [1967], the Court of Appeal held that *mens rea* was an essential ingredient in unlawful act manslaughter, and the *mens rea* is that of the base crime. In light of *Andrews* [2002], can it be suggested that unlawful act manslaughter might be an offence of strict liability if the base crime is too? You will find insight into this issue in the Commentary to the case in the *Criminal Law Review* of 2003 at 477.

Does D have to foresee harm or death? A quick reference to *DPP v Newbury and Jones* [1977] will reveal the answer to this question is 'no'.

The act must be dangerous

Revision tip

One of the common weaknesses in exam answers on constructive manslaughter is failure to explain the element of dangerousness. Sometimes it is often omitted entirely, but often it is misstated or the explanations given are incomplete. It is not a particularly difficult area of law, provided you learn the main cases cited in this section and apply the law to the question.

The unlawful act (ie the base crime) must be dangerous. So, what is the test of dangerousness?

Unlawful act manslaughter

****

Church [1966] 1 QB 59

This is the leading case, which we first examined in chapter 3. D had taken a woman to his van for sexual purposes and she mocked him for failing to satisfy her. During a fist fight between them, D knocked V semi-conscious. Thinking she was dead, D panicked and threw V into a river, where she died from drowning. On appeal against conviction, D argued (*inter alia*) that his act could not have been dangerous in his eyes, because throwing a dead body into a river cannot be dangerous to that body. The Court of Appeal dismissed his appeal. We cannot emphasise enough the importance of learning the test for dangerous in full:

> the unlawful act must be such as all sober and reasonable people would inevitably recognise must subject the other person to, at least, the risk of some (physical) harm resulting therefrom, albeit not serious harm.

The following two cases should be compared and contrasted, revised as illustrations of the *Church* test, but *not* confused with issues of causation.

Dawson (1985) 81 Cr App R 150

D robbed a 60-year-old garage attendant at midnight with a pickaxe handle and a replica gun. V suffered from heart disease. Shortly after the police arrived he collapsed and died from a heart attack. The Court of Appeal held that the *Church* test is based on the knowledge of the sober and reasonable person present at the scene. Such a person would not inevitably recognise a 60-year-old man as having a weak heart.

A common misconception is that in *Dawson*, D did not *cause* V to die. However, D's conviction was quashed due to jury misdirection.

Watson [1989] 1 WLR 684

Although there was no evidence that D knew the age or physical condition of V, during the course of a burglary of the home of a frail 87-year-old, D must have become aware of V's approximate age and frailty. Therefore, since a sober and reasonable bystander would also have become aware of those circumstances D's unlawful act was '*Church* dangerous'.

So, unless D has made an unreasonable mistake (and of course, the reasonable person does not make unreasonable mistakes (see *Ball* [1989])), the sober and reasonable person has all of D's knowledge, and all of the knowledge that a sober and reasonable person would ordinarily have. The test's purpose is to assess whether the act is dangerous; and it is *if*:

* a sober and reasonable person
* would inevitably recognise

- the act might subject V
- to the risk of some physical harm.

The act must cause V's death

The prosecution must prove D satisfies that *actus reus* of homicide (ie that D caused V to die). We have examined this in chapters 2 and 7 and will not repeat the law here other than to point out the importance of *Kennedy* [2008] in this context.

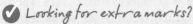

The Law Commission in its Report, *Legislating the Criminal Code: Involuntary Manslaughter* (Law Com No 237, 1996) recommended the abolition of the offence of constructive manslaughter because of the nature of constructive liability and also because of the lack of a requirement of foresight of harm. You might wish to read the report, but also note how the proposed new offence (see 'Reform', p 106) includes foresight to harm (but is still constructive in nature). This is particularly relevant to essay questions.

Gross negligence manslaughter

The leading case is *Adomako* [1995].

Adomako [1995] 1 AC 171

D was an anaesthetist who failed to notice when a patient's tube became disconnected from a ventilator. The patient suffered a cardiac arrest and died. The House of Lords held that in cases of manslaughter by criminal negligence involving a breach of duty, the ordinary principles of the law of negligence applied to ascertain whether D had been in breach of a duty of care towards V, whether it caused the death of V, and if so, whether it should be characterised as gross negligence and therefore a crime. Having regard to the risk of death involved, was D's conduct so bad in all the circumstances as to amount to a criminal act or omission?

Traditionally, this offence is phrased as a three-stage test (breach of a duty, causing death, very serious) but as this book is designed to simplify the basics (as well as stimulate thought for the higher marks), our advice is to learn it as a *five-stage test*, then you are far more likely to remember everything you need.

The five definitional elements

1. D owes V a duty of care.
2. D breaches that duty.

3. The breach involves an obvious risk of death.

4. The breach causes death.

5. And the jury finds the breach serious enough to be a crime (ie this is what makes it 'gross' negligence).

D owes V a duty of care

Most of the time, normal principles from the law of torts will dictate if there is a duty of care (see, eg *Donoghue v Stevenson* [1932], *Caparo v Dickman* [1990]), and if you have not yet studied the law of torts, take your guidance from your tutors on what you are expected to know. An example of a duty can be seen in *Winter* [2011], where D, who stored fireworks illegally, owed a duty to fire officers to tell them what was stored in the building.

Revision tip

1. Be aware that not all tortious duties will give rise to duties in the criminal law; see for example *Khan and Khan* [1998] in chapter 2, p 18. Compare that case with *Ruffell* [2003] and *Evans* [2009] in the same chapter, also on p 18.

2. Not all tortious principles are replicated in the criminal law; see *Wacker* [2003].

3. There is a tension between duties which exist in the civil law and those existing in the criminal law, best explained by Herring and Palser; see 'Key debates', p 109.

4. Although in *Singh* [1999] the Court of Appeal held that it is for the trial judge to rule if there is a duty of care, in *Willoughby* [2005] the court held the judge must only decide if there is sufficient evidence to establish a duty, and whether one does exist is a question for the jury.

One word of advice, we owe duties to avoid *acts* and *omissions*. The reason this is emphasised is because students sometimes think, wrongly, that gross negligence manslaughter arises only for omissions and that we do not owe a duty to avoid harmful acts, which of course we do.

D breaches that duty

Normal rules from the law of torts apply, so if D has done something (or not done something) and his conduct falls far below that of an ordinary person, the duty is breached.

The breach involves an obvious risk of death

This element is not found in the civil law and different levels of breach have been set in previous cases (eg in *Bateman* (1927), the breach of duty simply had to involve a disregard of the life and safety of others). It is now clear that the jury must be satisfied that the breach of duty involves an *obvious risk of death*.

Misra and Srivastava [2005] 1 Cr App R 21

Two doctors were convicted of the manslaughter of a patient who had died after contracting, and not receiving treatment for, a severe bacterial infection following a routine knee operation. The Court of Appeal held that the jury had been correctly directed that the negligent breach of that duty had exposed V to the risk of death; 'the circumstances must be such that a reasonably prudent person would have foreseen a serious and obvious risk not merely of injury, even serious injury, but of death'.

The prosecution does not have to prove that D knew his conduct involved a risk of death or that he foresaw the risk.

Mark [2004] EWCA Crim 2490

D was the managing director of a company that had a contract to clean a large storage tank. Acetone was used to clean the tank and, following an explosion, an employee suffered severe burns and subsequently died. D contended that he had been ignorant of the risk of using acetone. However, his appeal was dismissed. Actual foresight of a risk was not essential for gross negligence manslaughter.

The breach causes death

P must prove D caused V to die (see chapters 2 and 7 for the *actus reus* of homicide).

The jury finds the breach serious enough to be a crime (ie this is what makes it 'gross' negligence)

In *Adomako* [1994], Lord Mackay:

- made it clear that this element is a jury question;
- held that civil negligence is not enough and only gross negligence is criminal;
- did not define what is gross negligence;
- thought it would be unwise to attempt to categorise the types of conduct which may be gross negligence;
- acknowledged the circularity of the test;
- said, as it is a judgment on matters of degrees, and is a question of fact, the lack of a clear definition or categorisation was not fatal to the correctness of the test.

The circularity is illustrated in Figure 8.2.

Figure 8.2 Gross negligence—a circular test

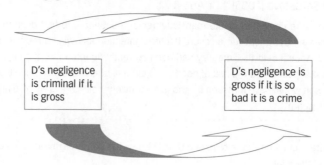

D's negligence is criminal if it is gross

D's negligence is gross if it is so bad it is a crime

Revision tip

Avoid a common mistake. Do not state that gross negligence manslaughter is a crime of strict liability. Why might you think it is?

1. There is no obvious *mens rea* word, eg knowingly or recklessly.

2. In *Attorney-General's Reference (No 2 of 1999)* [2000], the Court of Appeal held that proof of D's state of mind was not needed for a conviction of gross negligence manslaughter.

But you should not go from here to the conclusion that there is therefore no *mens rea* for gross negligence manslaughter. Remind yourself that *mens rea* should not be translated strictly as a 'guilty mind' but is better thought of as the fault element (or blameworthiness or culpability). Obviously the grossness of the negligence involves an assessment of fault, and that fault is assessed by examining the seriousness of D's conduct and the risks involved. It is objective, but it is *mens rea*.

In *Misra and Srivastava* [2005] on p 105, the Court of Appeal rejected the submission that this element of the offence lacked certainty and therefore breached **Article 7 ECHR** (which we mentioned, 'Influences of Europe' in chapter 1, p 8), stating that 'the question for the jury was not whether the defendant's negligence was gross and whether, *additionally*, it was a crime, but whether his behaviour was grossly negligent and *consequently* criminal' (emphasis added).

Reform

The Law Commission proposed in *Murder, manslaughter and infanticide* (Law Com No 304, 2006) to create a 'ladder' of homicide offences, including reformulating murder into first and second degree (see Figure 8.3). These are unlikely to be enacted, as the only changes so far have been to voluntary manslaughter (see chapter 7), but the proposals relating to unlawful act and gross negligence manslaughter are worthy of your consideration.

Figure 8.3 Unlawful homicide, Law Commission proposals in Law Com No 304

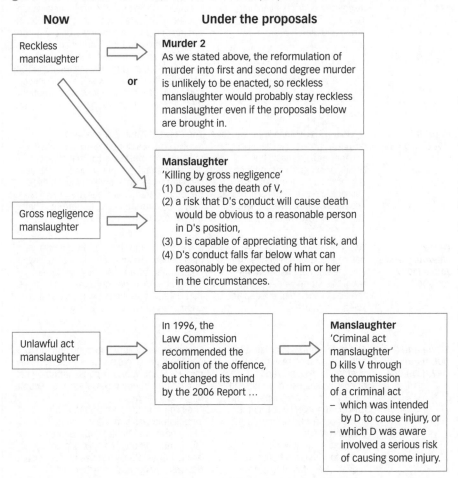

Key cases

Case	Facts	Principle
Adomako [1995] 1 AC 171	An anaesthetist failed to notice when a patient's tube became disconnected from a ventilator. The patient suffered a cardiac arrest and died.	In cases of manslaughter by criminal negligence involving a breach of duty, the ordinary principles of the law of negligence applied to ascertain whether D had been in breach of a duty of care towards V, whether it caused the death of V, and if so, whether it should be characterised as gross negligence and therefore a crime. Having regard to the risk of death involved, was D's conduct so bad in all the circumstances as to amount to a criminal act or omission?
Church [1966] 1 QB 59	D had taken a woman to his van for sexual purposes and she mocked him for failing to satisfy her. During a fist fight between them, D knocked V semi-conscious. Thinking she was dead, D panicked and threw V into a river, where she died from drowning.	The Court of Appeal dismissed his appeal. The test for dangerous is that the unlawful act must be such that all sober and reasonable people would inevitably recognise it as an act which must subject the other person to at least the risk of some (physical) harm resulting therefrom, albeit not serious harm.
DPP v Newbury and Jones [1977] AC 500	Two 15-year-old boys pushed a paving stone over a bridge and into the path of the oncoming train. The stone went through the glass window of the cab and killed the guard.	It is manslaughter if it is proved that D intentionally did an act which was unlawful and dangerous and that act inadvertently caused death. It was unnecessary to prove that D knew that the act was unlawful or dangerous or whether D recognised its danger.
Stone and Dobinson [1977] QB 354	The defendants, a partially deaf and almost blind man of below average intelligence and no appreciable sense of smell, and his partner, who was ineffectual and inadequate, lived together in his house with his mentally subnormal son. The man's anorexic sister, V, came to live at the house as a lodger. She refused to eat and rejected the defendants' (limited) assistance. V died from toxemia spreading from infected bed scores, prolonged immobilisation, and lack of food.	On the facts the jury had been entitled to find the defendants had assumed a duty to care for V and were obliged to summon help or care for V themselves when she became helplessly infirm. The breach of duty which had to be established was a reckless disregard of danger to her health and welfare by indifference to an obvious risk of injury to health or by actually foreseeing the risk and determining nevertheless to run it.

Key debates

Topic	'Legislating the criminal code: involuntary manslaughter'
Author/Academic	The Law Commission
Viewpoint	For a detailed analysis of the common law, see in particular Parts III (What is wrong with the present law) and IV (The moral basis of criminal liability for unintentionally causing death). You should read this in conjunction with the 2006 report (pp 3–9, 19–24, 50–51, and 61–64), bearing in mind the changes that have been made in respect of voluntary manslaughter under the **Coroners and Justice Act 2009** (see chapter 7).
Source	Law Com No 237 (1996) and Law Com No 304 (2006)

Topic	'The duty of care in gross negligence manslaughter'
Author/Academic	Jonathan Herring and Elaine Palser
Viewpoint	Examines the meaning of duty of care in the law of torts and the criminal law; comparing and critiquing case law on each area. Also debates whether it is, and should be, a question for the judge or jury.
Source	[2007] Crim LR 24

Exam questions

Problem question

At a school swimming lesson held at a public sports centre, Alicia, aged ten, died as a result of drowning. Discuss whether any of the following people may be criminally liable for her manslaughter by gross negligence:

1. Robert, who was Alicia's teacher. Robert knew Alicia was a weak swimmer but had forgotten to bring armbands to the class that day.
2. Carly, who was the lifeguard at the leisure centre. At the time when Alicia got into difficulties and drowned, Carly was not in the pool area, because she had gone to the lavatory. Carly forgot to tell Robert that she would be absent for a few minutes. It is a term of Carly's contract that whenever a lifeguard had to be absent from the pool, an adult would be informed.
3. David, a member of the public, who was using the leisure centre facilities that day and who saw Alicia was in trouble in the water. David is a strong swimmer. David did not assist Alicia.

Would your answer to 3 be different if David had helped Alicia, but when David gave Alicia mouth-to-mouth resuscitation, he in fact pushed too hard on her chest causing her ribs to crack and her lung to burst, and Alicia died as a result of the injuries caused by David rather than by drowning?

An outline answer is included at the end of the book.

Essay question

> It should not be possible to convict a person for any homicide in the absence of proof of foresight of any harm to the victim.

Critically evaluate the offences of involuntary manslaughter in light of this statement.

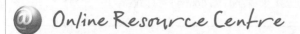

To see an outline answer to this question log on to www.oxfordtextbooks.co.uk/orc/concentrate/

#9

Inchoate offences

- Inchoate means 'just begun' or 'incomplete'. Inchoate offences are those where the full offence is not completed.

- The reason that the law fixes liability on defendants who have not fulfilled the full offence is to punish those who are willing to be involved in criminality even where the full offence is not, for one reason or another, completed.

- The common law offence of **incitement** was replaced with new offences under the **Serious Crime Act 2007**. The law governing **conspiracy** and attempts was the subject of a Law Commission Consultation Paper (2007) and report in December 2009, *Conspiracy and Attempts* (Law Com No 318, 2009).

- Reforms, both actual and proposed, are complex and piecemeal, but they serve to highlight what is wrong with the present law, and how the Law Commission sees the law improving.

Chapter overview

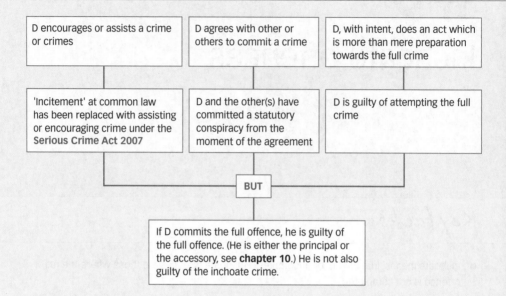

D encourages or assists a crime or crimes

D agrees with other or others to commit a crime

D, with intent, does an act which is more than mere preparation towards the full crime

'Incitement' at common law has been replaced with assisting or encouraging crime under the **Serious Crime Act 2007**

D and the other(s) have committed a statutory conspiracy from the moment of the agreement

D is guilty of attempting the full crime

BUT

If D commits the full offence, he is guilty of the full offence. (He is either the principal or the accessory, see **chapter 10**.) He is not also guilty of the inchoate crime.

Introduction

It is possible to study the topics in chapter 10 *without* studying the offences covered here, but in light of recent changes to the law, it is very unwise to study the offences *here* without having some understanding of accessorial liability in chapter 10.

Inchoate liability is liability for an incomplete crime. Inchoate liability is often justified because D has demonstrated a willingness to be involved in, to assist or encourage, or to take the steps towards a crime. If the full offence is carried out *by D*, he may be liable as the perpetrator, but will not be liable for the inchoate offence as well. If the full offence is carried out *by another*, D may be liable as an accessory for the principal offence. Inchoate liability exists separately to either of these types of liability.

Assisting or encouraging

The common law offence of incitement was replaced with three statutory offences consisting of assisting or encouraging crime contrary to **ss 44–46 Serious Crime Act 2007**, based on the Law Commission's proposals in *Inchoate liability for assisting and encouraging crime* (Law Com No 300, 2006). D is liable whether or not the full crime is subsequently committed.

The three new offences are:

- intentionally encouraging or assisting an offence (**s 44**);
- encouraging or assisting an offence believing it will be committed (**s 45**); and
- encouraging or assisting offences believing one or more will be committed (**s 46**).

The *mens rea* requirements are found in **s 47** in respect of what D believes or intends the other (P) to do and P's state of mind at that time.

In *Sadique* [2013], the Court of Appeal considered the ingredients of the **s 46** offence, and summarised them at [34]:

(a) D must be involved in an act

(b) D must be capable of assisting another/others to commit a crime, but (a) and (b) are not criminal unless

(c) D believed what he was doing would encourage or assist the other(s) in the commission of crimes and

(d) D also believed that was the purpose or one of the purposes of his act of involvement.

See also Table 9.1.

Conspiracy
****

Table 9.1 Assisting or encouraging crime

	Section 44	Section 45	Section 46
Actus reus	D does an act capable of encouraging or assisting the commission of an offence.	D does an act capable of encouraging or assisting the commission of an offence.	D does an act capable of encouraging or assisting the commission of one or more of a number of offences.
Mens rea	D intends to encourage or assist its commission.	D believes that the offence will be committed and that his act will encourage or assist its commission.	D believes that one or more of those offences will be committed (but has no belief as to which) and that his act will encourage or assist the commission of one or more of them.

Revision tip

Section 51 Serious Crime Act 2007 provides that certain parties cannot be convicted of the assisting and encouraging offences outlined previously if they are the 'victims' of a protected offence. You should be able to illustrate who might fall within that category.

Section 50 Serious Crime Act 2007 provides D with a defence of reasonable action (s 50(1)) or reasonable belief (s 50(2)). The burden of proof lies on D. The first defence would cover, for example, undercover police officers, and the second might cover, for example, a person driving at 70 mph in the outside lane of the motorway, who pulls over to allow a speeding motorist to pass (see 'Key debates', on p 118).

✔ *Looking for extra marks?*

The offence under s 46 was considered in *Sadique* [2012]. The appellants argued the offence was too uncertain and vague and therefore breached Art 7 ECHR. The Court of Appeal rejected the argument, but in so doing, emphasised the narrow scope of the offence to those which D thinks *will* happen as opposed to those which he thinks *might*. For an analysis of the case, see the 2013 *Archbold Review*, volume 7, pp 4–6.

Conspiracy

There are two types of conspiracy: statutory conspiracy under the Criminal Law Act 1977, and common law conspiracy, consisting of conspiracy to defraud (examined in chapter 12) and conspiracy to do acts tending to corrupt public morals or outrage public decency.

Statutory conspiracy

Section 1 Criminal Law Act 1977 provides:

(1) ... if a person agrees with any other person or persons that a course of conduct shall be pursued which, if the agreement is carried out in accordance with their intentions, either—

(a) will necessarily amount to or involve the commission of any offence or offences by one or more of the parties to the agreement, or

(b) would do so but for the existence of facts which render the commission of the offence or any of the offences impossible,

he is guilty of conspiracy to commit the offence or offences in question.

Actus reus

- An agreement (if two or more people agree to carry a criminal scheme into effect, the crime is the agreement itself). Nothing need be done in pursuit of the agreement.

- As to a course of conduct. There may even be an element of reservation as to the conduct to be pursued, such as 'We will beat up a policeman if he is at the scene.' (See also *Jackson* [1985].)

Mens rea

The leading case of *Anderson* [1986] (see 'Key cases', p 118). The current *mens rea* for statutory conspiracy is intention to be a party to an agreement and intention that the substantive offence be carried out by one of the conspirators (even if it is impossible, and even if D knew what was planned and failed to stop it, *Siracusa* (1990)).

If the proposals in the Law Commission Report No 318 are enacted, *Anderson* will be repealed and the *mens rea* will be that D and at least one other party intend or are at least reckless to the conduct elements of the offence plus intend or are at least reckless to any relevant consequences, and this applies even if the *mens rea* in the substantive offence is negligence, or if there is no *mens rea* in respect of that element in the substantive offence (ie it is strict liability).

Revision tip

Certain parties cannot be convicted of conspiracy and these include the intended victim and the spouse or civil partner of the other party (**s 2 Criminal Law Act 1977**). The Law Commission has recommended the abolition of the spousal privilege. Why? This is the sort of area of law that is useful to know in case there is an essay question comparing present law with the Law Commission proposals.

Common law conspiracy

The common law offence of conspiracy to defraud is considered in chapter 12.

It is a crime at common law to conspire to corrupt public morals (*Shaw v DPP* [1962]) and it is also a crime to conspire to outrage public decency (*Knuller v DPP* [1973]). As they rarely feature in examination questions in their own right, we advise you to refer to a criminal law textbook should these crimes be a major part of your programme.

Attempts

Section 1 Criminal Attempts Act 1981 provides:

1. If, with intent to commit an offence ... a person does an act which is more than merely preparatory to the commission of the offence, he is guilty of attempting to commit the offence...

2 A person may be guilty of attempting to commit an offence to which this section applies even though the facts are such that the commission of the offence is impossible.

Actus reus

Where the line is between an act (not an omission) done in preparation and an act which is *more than merely preparatory* is one of fact, and accordingly it has caused some apparently inconsistent decisions.

....

Jones [1990] 1 WLR 1057

D had committed attempted murder even though there were at least three more steps before the full offence could have been completed (removing the safety catch of the sawn-off shotgun that he was pointing at V, putting his finger on the trigger, and pulling it). The Court of Appeal held that 'more than merely preparatory' does not mean the last act within D's power. However, in *Gullefer* [1990], D had not gone beyond the stage of mere preparation when he ran on a track in an effort to have the greyhound race, on which D had placed a bet which he was going to lose, abandoned.

....

....

Geddes [1996] Crim LR 894

D was found in a school toilet with a knife, string, and sealing tape. His conviction for attempted false imprisonment was quashed. Although D clearly had the intention, he had not made any contact with pupils and had gone no further than the preparatory stages of the offence. And again in *Campbell* (1991), D argued successfully that even though he had intended to rob the post office (he was in possession of a gun and a demand note) he had changed his mind before going in, and was arrested before he had a chance to depart the area.

....

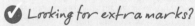

It is for the judge to rule whether there is any evidence capable of constituting an attempt, and for the jury to say whether it accepts this as amounting to an attempt.

Mens rea

Because an attempt is, by definition, not the full offence, it is the *mens rea* that is crucial because it can turn an apparent accident into a crime.

The *mens rea* for attempts is:

- intention in respect of the conduct or the consequences of *the full offence*; and
- (where the full offence is defined as recklessness in respect of any circumstances) recklessness in respect of any circumstances (*Khan* [1990]).

Note: Because the *mens rea* is intention to commit the *full* offence, the *mens rea* of attempted murder is intention to kill, even though the *mens rea* of murder is intention to kill or intention to cause really serious harm. Make sure you understand this, for each attempted crime you have to consider.

Attempting the impossible

The leading case on whether D can be liable for attempting a crime which is impossible to commit is *Shivpuri* [1987] which is in 'Key cases', p 118.

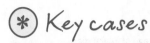

Key cases

Case	Facts	Principle
Anderson [1986] AC 27	D and X were on remand in prison. They spent one night in the same cell. D expected shortly to be released on bail, and agreed with X that D would get some wire cutters and give them to a third party. After he was released, though, D was involved in a car accident and could not assist. D later said he had never intended that the escape plan should be carried into effect nor believed that it could possibly succeed.	The House of Lords dismissed his appeal against conviction for conspiracy. It was not necessary to establish an intention on the part of each conspirator that the offence or offences in question should in fact be committed; it was sufficient to show that he had known that the course of conduct to be pursued would amount to the commission of an offence and that he had intended to play some part in the agreed course of conduct in furtherance of the criminal purpose that it had been intended to achieve.
Shivpuri [1987] AC 1	D was carrying a package containing a powdered substance which he thought was a controlled drug. He was charged with various offences of attempted drug dealing, but an analysis of the substance found proved it to be merely vegetable material.	Lord Bridge, dismissing D's appeal against conviction, held that in respect of **s 1 Criminal Attempts Act 1981** the jury should consider two questions (and notwithstanding that the commission of the actual offence was, on the facts impossible): 1. Did the defendant intend to commit the offence which it is alleged he attempted to commit? 2. Did he, in relation to that offence, do an act which was more than merely preparatory to the commission of the *intended offence*?

Key debates

Topic	Serious Crime Act 2007: The Part 2 offences
Author/Academic	D Ormerod and R Fortson
Viewpoint	The authors greeted the **Serious Crime Act 2007** with a 'lack of enthusiasm' per Lord Judge CJ in *Sadique* [2013].
Sources	[2009] Crim LR 389

Topic	'Encouraging or assisting crime'
Author/Academic	L Leigh
Viewpoint	This is a useful summary and critique of the provisions of **Pt 2 Serious Crime Act 2007**.
Source	[2008] *Archbold News* 6

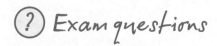

⑦ Exam questions

Problem question

Paul was a loan shark, which means he lent money to people who needed it, but at a very high rate of interest. Ron borrowed a substantial amount of money from Paul and he was unable to repay it. Paul told Ron that he (Ron) must pay off his debts including the interest to Paul immediately or he must agree to 'beat up' Mark, a man who also owed Paul money and who had refused to repay it.

Ron did not have any money to repay Paul, so he agreed to beat up Mark. Ron's brother, Sam, was a very large-built and strong man. Ron enlisted Sam's help.

Ron and Sam went to Mark's house and broke in. Mark was watching the television. When Mark saw Ron and Sam, he had a heart attack and died immediately. Ron and Sam ran from the scene but were arrested outside Mark's house by police officers.

Consider the liability of Paul, Ron, and Sam as follows:

1. Paul for intentionally encouraging the offence of causing grievous bodily harm with intent, contrary to **s 44 Serious Crime Act 2007,**

2. Paul and Ron for conspiracy to commit grievous bodily harm with intent, and

3. Ron and Sam for attempting to commit grievous bodily harm with intent.

An outline answer is included at the end of the book.

Essay question

A defendant who attempts a crime must do the very last act dependent on him before he can be convicted. This is clearly too late, especially as that person will already have formed a culpable *mens rea*.

Critically analyse whether the law governing attempts is satisfactory, in light of this comment.

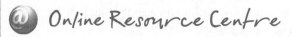

ⓦ Online Resource Centre

To see an outline answer to this question log on to www.oxfordtextbooks.co.uk/orc/concentrate/

#10
Participation

- The liability of parties who participate in the criminal acts of others can be split into four parts; those who are accessories, those who are joint perpetrators, those vicariously liable, and those who are corporations.

- Accessories are those who **aid, abet, counsel or procure** the commission of the principal offence. Such **accessories** (referred to in this chapter as A) are *charged* as if they committed the crime themselves.

- Although the accessories are charged as principals, the *actus reus* and *mens rea* requirements of the accessories are different.

- Participants who enter a **joint venture** (also known as a joint unlawful enterprise) are liable for the crimes committed as part of that venture, unless one of the parties deliberately departs from the agreed plan. In that case, the liability of the other depends on his foresight of the departed act.

- The process of identifying the principal offence is vital because the liability of the other participants derives from the offence the principal has committed.

- The doctrine of vicarious liability has a (limited) role in the criminal law.

- A corporation is a legal person, so criminal liability can be imposed on a corporation for many (although not all) crimes.

Chapter overview

This is the **principal** (P). He has committed a crime, and this is the principal offence. His liability for the principal offence **does not** concern us, but we do need to be aware of what the principal offence is because the liability of the accessories is for the **same** offence.

This is the **accessory** (A). He has aided, abetted, counselled, or procured the principal offence. His liability for the principal offence **does** concern us.

This is the **joint venturer** (JV). He has joined in the principal offence with P. Where the plan is fulfilled, P and JV are each convicted of the principal offence, and the matter is simple. But the law is more complex where P has departed from the agreed plan. What then of JV's liability?

This is an employer or corporation. Where an employee (P) has committed a criminal offence can the employer or corporation (A) be liable (as well as P, or instead of P) for that crime?

Introduction

The law studied here is complicated, and although this puts many students off studying this topic, we hope to reassure you; it is not your job to solve the complications and inconsistencies of the law, but to learn them and show you understand them in the exam. In this chapter, we are concerned with the liability of those who participate before or during the criminal act of another. We start with two important notes on terminology. First:

- **P** in this chapter stands for principal or perpetrator. Other than for cases of innocent agents, P is the person who brings about the *actus reus* of the principal offence. You must always identify the principal offence first; the criminal liability of the others depends on it.
- **A** stands for accessory.
- **JV** stands for joint venturer.

Secondly: In chapter 9 we examined inchoate liability which is the liability of parties for criminal offences where the principal offence is *not* (necessarily) committed. Here we are examining accessorial/participation liability. The principal offence *has* been committed (indeed if it has not, there is no accessorial liability at all) and we are examining the liability of those who help, encourage, or join in.

Please note that the cases we examine are factually complex because they each involve at least three parties (P, V, and A), but they are important because A's liability depends on what P did to V, and what A thought about what P might do.

Revision tip

In order to be able to answer either an essay or a problem question on accessories you are strongly urged to have read at least one of the standard textbooks on this topic before you start to compile your revision notes. You will also find it useful to practise writing answers (in timed conditions) to your tutorial/seminar questions or past papers.

The *actus reus* of accessorial liability

An accessory in English law is a person who assists P before or during the crime. However (and this is vital) the accessory is *charged as the principal*. Section 8 Accessories and Abettors Act 1861 provides:

> Whosoever shall aid, abet, counsel, or procure the commission of [an ... offence] ... shall be liable to be tried, indicted, and punished as a principal offender.

What does this mean? Say P is charged with burglary and the details of the burglary are that he broke into and stole property from V's home. Say further that A acted as a lookout and getaway driver. A is also charged with burglary (exactly the same as P) but in the particulars of the offence it will specify that A aided (and/or abetted and/or counselled and/or procured) the burglary. The indictment may therefore read as stated in Figure 10.1.

Figure 10.1 'Tried, indicted and punished as a principal'

IN THE CROWN COURT AT NORCHESTER

THE QUEEN

V

P and A

Statement of Offence

That P committed burglary contrary to section 9(1)(a) of the Theft Act 1968, A being aider and abettor to same offence.

Particulars of Offence

P, on the 4th day of July 2013, entered as a trespasser a building, being a dwelling known as number 20 Smith Road Norchester, with intent to steal therein, and that A, at the same time and place did aid and abet, counsel and procure P to commit the said offence.

The prosecution has to prove that P committed burglary and A either aided, abetted, counselled, or procured that principal offence.

Although the use of the four words in the 1861 Act (aid, etc) indicates that there must be a difference between them (if there was none, why would four words have been used?), the Court of Appeal in *Bryce* [2004] suggested that all four should be used in the particulars to avoid wrongful acquittals arising from any technicality in the words used.

Revision tip

In answering problem questions, it is good practice to identify on the facts whether A has aided, abetted, counselled, or procured, using cases in illustration. You will probably discover, however, that the more contentious issue is whether A satisfies the *mens rea*.

Aid

It is generally thought that aiding means helping or giving assistance to the perpetrator before or at the time of the commission of the offence.

Tuck v Robson [1970] 1 WLR 741

A (a pub landlord) aided and abetted when he permitted customers to continue drinking alcohol after the licensing hours. However, in *Clarkson* [1971], A's mere presence at the scene of a crime, where there was no duty to prevent the crime, was not aiding. There has to be evidence of assistance or encouragement (and an intention that A's act would assist or encourage).

Abet

Although there is no authoritative case law definition on the meaning of abetting, it is generally seen as meaning encouraging, instigating, or inciting the commission of the crime by a person present at the scene of the crime. See *Stringer* [2012].

Wilcox v Jeffery [1951] 1 All ER 464

An American saxophone player (P) was given permission to land in England on the condition that he took no employment, paid or unpaid, in the UK. A, a magazine editor, knew of the condition imposed, but attended a concert where P played his saxophone and afterwards A published a glowing review of the concert. A had abetted P.

Counsel

To counsel means to advise or solicit and is usually done before the crime and the counsellor is not present at the scene. There is no need to prove the counselling caused the offence (*Giannetto* [1997]).

Calhaem [1985] QB 808

A was said to have hired P to murder another woman, V. P had already pleaded guilty to murder, and gave evidence at A's trial. P said although A had hired him to kill V, he had originally resolved not to do so, but at the scene he went berserk and killed V. A was convicted of counselling V's murder. She had instructed and authorised P to kill V and P had acted within the scope of that authority. There was no need to prove a causal connection between the counselling and the principal crime.

Procure

To procure means to *cause* (*Stringer* [2012]) or 'to produce by endeavour'.

AG's Ref (No 1 of 1975) [1975] QB 773

A secretly laced P's drinks, knowing P would shortly be driving home. This was procuring P's offence of drink driving. There was a causal connection between A's acts and the principal crime, and A foresaw the principal crime. Lord Widgery CJ held: 'You procure a thing by setting out to see that it happens and taking the appropriate steps to produce that happening.'

The *mens rea* of accessorial liability

The following is a summary from the decision in *Bryce* [2004]:

A intentionally assists P

+

A knows his assistance is for P to commit a crime (the principal offence)

+

A knows there is a real possibility that P might commit the crime
(that is, A foresees the principal offence)

Intentionally assisting P

This is best explained by an example:

....

National Coal Board v Gamble [1959] 1 QB 11

A worked at a weighbridge. He weighed a lorry driven by P and he told P that the lorry was over the regulation weight (a criminal offence). P replied that he would take the risk. A then gave P a receipt for the weighbridge. P was caught and A was charged with aiding and abetting the offence. The Divisional Court held that the crime of aiding and abetting was committed on proof of a positive act of assistance (giving P the ticket) voluntarily done, and a knowledge of the circumstances constituting the offence (knowing the lorry was over the regulation weight).

....

And foresight of the commission of the principal offence

You will see this element variously referred to as consisting of foresight, contemplation, or 'knowledge of the essential matters', but in essence this test is whether D realised as a real possibility that P might commit the principal offence. As Sir Robin Cooke explained in *Chan Wing Sui* [1985], A's liability 'turns on *contemplation*. It meets the case of a crime *foreseen* as a possible incident of the common unlawful enterprise. The criminal culpability lies in participating in the venture *with that foresight*' (emphasis added).

So, the prosecution must prove foresight, but foresight of what? Either:

- that P might commit an offence *of the type* actually committed by P (*Bainbridge* [1960], see 'Key cases', p 131); *or*

- that P might commit an offence *within a range* of a limited number of crimes that A contemplated P might commit (*Maxwell* [1978] see 'Key cases', p 132).

Derivative liability

A's criminal liability depends on proof that the principal crime occurred, or at least the *actus reus* of the principal offence.

Derivative liability

✱✱✱✱✱✱✱✱✱✱

Thornton v Mitchell [1940] 1 All ER 339

P was a bus driver who was charged with driving without due care and attention. P had reversed a bus and two pedestrians were knocked down. P had relied on the directions of the conductor (A) so therefore P had not driven without due care and attention. He *had* paid attention, albeit to what A had carelessly told him. A could therefore not be convicted of aiding and abetting the principal offence because P had not committed the principal offence.

If you can grasp this case, and explain it to a non-lawyer (a parent, friend, pet, whoever), you have grasped the nature of derivative liability. Do not proceed until you understand this first fundamental step. If the *actus reus* of the principal offence is satisfied, A may be convicted of aiding (etc) it, even if P is not.

Cogan and Leak [1976] QB 217

A (the husband) terrorised V (his wife) into having sexual intercourse with another man (P). P was acquitted (because he lacked *mens rea* as he believed the sexual intercourse was consensual) but A's conviction was upheld by the Court of Appeal. A's liability was derivative not on the *guilt* of P but on the commission of the *actus reus* of the principal offence. See also *Millward* [1994].

✅ Looking for extra marks?

The *obiter dictum* in **Cogan and Leak** [1976] to the effect that A could have been charged as P (P simply being an innocent agent) is controversial not least because, if correct, it could mean that a woman could be convicted of rape as principal offender. You could use this point in an essay asking for your evaluation of the nature of derivative liability.

If P is not guilty because he has a defence, A may still be guilty (*Bourne* (1952)). It is possible for A to be liable for a different offence from P, provided the offences have a shared *actus reus*. In *Howe* [1987], Lord Mackay explained that if A gave a gun to P, informing him that it was loaded with blanks and telling him to go and scare V by firing it, but the ammunition was in fact live (and A knew it was live) and V was killed, even if P was convicted as perpetrator, it could only be for manslaughter because he lacked intention to kill or cause GBH. A would nonetheless be guilty of aiding and abetting murder.

Revision tip

You may have to cross-reference your studies on derivative liability to the new offences of assisting or encouraging crime in chapter 9, especially 'Assisting or encouraging', pp 113 and 114. Three new offences have been created in the **Serious Crime Act 2007** where D may be convicted whether the P offence *is subsequently committed or not*.

Joint venture liability

We now consider a topic which falls within the law already examined, but with an extra complication. If A and JV agree to commit crime X, and they commit crime X, each is guilty of crime X, and we do not have to be concerned with this any further. However, if A and JV agree to commit crime X, but JV departs from the plan and commits crime Y, is A liable for crime Y? As we shall see, crime Y is often murder and crime X is often a crime of violence, and the complication arises because the *mens rea* for murder (as principal) is intention to kill *or* cause serious harm. The leading cases are *Powell* [1999] and *English* [1999], heard together at the House of Lords.

Powell [1999] 1 AC 1

This was an appeal in the case of the murder of a drug dealer, who had been shot by one of a group of three men. The prosecution could not prove who had actually fired the gun but each member of the group knew of the existence of the gun. The House of Lords held that where A contemplates that JV might kill with intent to do so or to cause really serious injury, A may be convicted as a secondary party to the murder, even though this means imposing a lower level of *mens rea* in relation to A than would have to be proved in relation to JV. In *English* [1999], A appealed against his conviction of the murder of a police officer who had been stabbed by JV with a knife while both A and JV were attacking the victim with wooden posts. A did not know JV was in possession of a knife. The House of Lords held that the question is what act A foresaw JV might commit. If JV committed an act which was fundamentally different from that which they jointly contemplated, he could not be guilty of murder or manslaughter unless the weapon used was just as dangerous as that which was contemplated.

The House of Lords revisited the decisions in *Powell* [1999] and *English* [1999] in *Rahman* [2008]. The legal complexity arises because, as you can see in Figure 10.2, A can be liable for murder if JV killed and A foresaw as a real possibility that JV might cause V GBH.

A is guilty of murder if A participated in the enterprise, and foresaw in the course of it that JV *might* kill either with intent to kill or intent to cause GBH (see *Willett* (2011) and *R v A* (2011)). A is guilty of manslaughter if he foresaw JV might cause non-serious injury, even if JV kills with either intent to kill or intent to cause GBH. But if the act JV committed is fundamentally different from the act A foresaw, A is not guilty.

Yemoh [2009] Crim LR 888

A, JV, and others were involved in a fight with other youths. A knew one of his group had a Stanley knife and intended to kill or cause GBH; but the fatal blow was struck with a longer knife with a pointed blade. This was not fundamentally different from the foreseen use of the Stanley knife (with the foreseen *mens rea*). Although a Stanley knife is not an efficient way to cause injury or kill, it can be used to this end if used in a slashing motion.

Joint venture liability
✷✷✷✷✷✷✷✷✷✷

Figure 10.2 *Rahman* [2008]: A's foresight of P's act

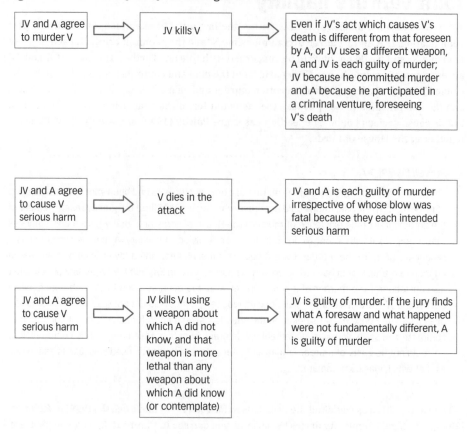

Liability for a lesser offence?

If A foresaw a fundamentally different act, he is not guilty of the principal crime, but he cannot necessarily escape liability for his *own* acts. As we saw previously, A might be convicted of a lesser crime if A satisfies the *actus reus* and *mens rea* of that crime as an individual (so A is now P of the other crime and not A to the principal crime).

In *Day* [2001], P was convicted of murder, and A of manslaughter, each on the basis of what they foresaw. The Commentary to the case (at [2001] Crim LR 984) explains some of the factual and legal complications arising from this outcome.

Put simply, the law governing participation is widely considered as being too widely drawn. One issue is that D's acts of encouragement and assistance do not have to *cause* the principal offence. Another is that A can be convicted on the basis of *foresight* when JV may be convicted only on proof of intent (eg murder) but A is liable as principal. Make sure you understand these views and are able to illustrate them by case examples.

Accessory or joint principal?

If we define an accessory as someone who assists before or at the scene, but the *actus reus* of the principal offence is carried out by another; and a joint venturer as someone who accompanies and does complete the *actus reus*, at least in part, are accessories and joint venturers different in law? The most recent decisions apply the same law (see *Rahman* [2008] and *Stringer* [2012]) and note that it tends to be only where JV commits murder in a departure from the agreement with A that complications arise, but it is *not* to be treated as a separate area of law. There may be criminal liability as an accessory, even to murder, where there is no joint venture on the facts (*Gnango* [2012]), but that does not mean the law underlying accessories and joint ventures is different.

Withdrawal from participation

It is possible, but not easy, for an accessory to withdraw from the criminal enterprise, provided he communicates the withdrawal to his associates, so that they know that they are now proceeding alone (see *Becerra* (1975), where running off and shouting 'let's go' were not sufficient).

....

Whitefield (1984) 79 Cr App R 36

A agreed with others to commit a burglary. A later changed his mind and told the others, but they continued as planned. A's appeal against conviction for burglary was allowed. He had served unequivocal notice on the others of withdrawing his aid and assistance.

....

The more A has contributed to the plan, the more he has to do to withdraw. In *Rook* (1993), simply not turning up was not enough. That said, if the joint venture was spontaneous, the withdrawal can be too (*Mitchell* [1999]), unless A initiated the venture, then he would have to do rather more (*Robinson* [2000]).

Vicarious liability

The principle of autonomy reflects the notion that we can choose how and when to act, and we *are individually responsible* for our actions. We are therefore not criminally responsible for another's actions unless we do something which assists them. This can be contrasted with the law of torts where vicarious liability is used to make an employer liable for the wrongful acts of his employee. It is an economically justifiable doctrine in torts law because it allows a wronged party to be compensated by the party best able to pay the compensation. However, the same cannot be true of criminal law because there is no compensation and each person involved in criminality is punished individually.

The criminal law has recognised *some* vicarious liability. It is limited to statutory crimes and is wholly a matter of statutory construction. The leading cases are:

- *Coppen v Moore (No 2)* [1898]: shop owner liable for employee's false trade description notwithstanding express instructions to the contrary.
- *Harrow LBC v Shah* [2000]: see chapter 4.
- *Allen v Whitehead* [1930]: owner of a café liable where employee to whom operation of the business had been delegated allowed prostitutes to congregate on the premises.

You should also be aware of the criticisms of the doctrine, best expressed by Lord Reid in *Vane v Yiannopoullos* [1965].

Corporate liability

A corporation is an artificial legal person. Just as a person can be criminally liable, so too can a corporation, but how are we to find the *actus reus* and the *mens rea* of the corporation? The answer is to apply the *identification doctrine*. Denning LJ explained this doctrine in *Bolton v Graham* [1957]. He said we can liken a corporation to a human body. The corporation's brain and nerve centre, which control what it does, are the directors and managers. They represent the corporation's directing mind and will, and it is here we will find its *mens rea*: the state of mind of these managers is the state of mind of the company and is treated by the law as such.

. . . .

Tesco v Nattrass [1972] AC 153

The question for the courts was whether the company was criminally liable when the manager of a supermarket applied a false trade description. The House of Lords held that the identification doctrine was not satisfied. Normally the board of directors, the managing director, and other superior officers of a company carry out the functions of management and speak and act as the company. Their subordinates, including store managers, do not.

. . . .

✔ *Looking for extra marks?*

Each of the Law Lords in *Tesco v Nattrass* [1972] agreed with the outcome, but differed in his explanation of who might amount to the 'directing mind' of the company. The difficulty their Lordships encountered should illustrate the complexity of the test.

There are certain crimes that a corporation cannot commit; murder (because of the sentence—a corporation cannot serve a prison sentence) and rape (because of the physical impossibility of such a crime), for example. But it was confirmed in the trial arising out of the sinking of the *Herald of Free Enterprise* that a corporation can be convicted of manslaughter, but only where an individual identified as the controlling mind of the company was also guilty; see also *AG's Ref (No 2 of 1999)* [2000].

Manslaughter by a corporation is now governed by the Corporate Manslaughter and Corporate Homicide Act 2007. A corporation commits an offence if the way in which its activities are managed or organised by senior management causes a death and amounts to a gross breach of a relevant duty of care owed to the deceased. For a recent case example, see *Cotswold Geotechnical (Holdings)* [2011].

Revision tip

If you are studying corporate manslaughter, we refer you to (among many others):

- D Ormerod and R Taylor, 'The Corporate Manslaughter and Corporate Homicide Act 2007' [2008] Crim LR 589
- J Gobert, 'The Corporate Manslaughter and Corporate Homicide Act 2007—thirteen years in the making but was it worth the wait?' (2008) 71(3) MLR 413–33
- A Dobson, 'Shifting Sands: multiple counts in prosecutions for corporate manslaughter' [2012] Crim LR 200.

(✱) *Key cases*

Case	Facts	Principle
Bainbridge [1960] 1 QB 129	A supplied P with oxyacetylene cutting equipment. A admitted he foresaw P doing something illegal but denied knowledge of the precise details. The equipment was used to break into a bank.	The Court of Appeal dismissed A's appeal against conviction for being an accessory. It is not enough to show that A knows that some illegal venture is intended; however where A knows that a crime of the type in question was intended and does an act intending to assist a crime of the type later committed, A may be convicted as an accessory to the crime.
English [1999] 1 AC 1, conjoined with Powell	A appealed against his conviction of the murder of a police officer who had been stabbed by JV with a knife while both A and JV were attacking the victim with wooden posts. A did not know JV was in possession of a knife.	If A did not foresee that JV might commit an act which was fundamentally different from that which they jointly contemplated, he could not be guilty of murder or manslaughter unless the weapon used was just as dangerous as that which was contemplated.

Key debates

✱✱✱✱✱✱✱✱✱✱✱

Case	Facts	Principle
Maxwell [1978] 1 WLR 1350	A was a member of a terrorist organisation. He guided P in his car to a public house where P threw a bomb. A appealed against his conviction for various offences relating to explosives.	The House of Lords rejected his appeal. A knew he was guiding terrorists, he knew the destination, and that weapons were to be used. As Lord Fraser explained, 'the possible extent of [A's] guilt was limited to the range of crimes any of which he must have known were to be expected'.
Powell [1999] 1 AC 1	A drug dealer had been shot by one of a group of three men. The prosecution could not prove who had actually fired the gun but they each knew of the existence of the gun.	Where A contemplates that JV might kill with intent to do so or to cause really serious injury, A may be convicted as a secondary party to the murder, even though this means imposing a lower level of *mens rea* in relation to A than would have to be proved in relation to JV.
Rahman [2009] 1 AC 129	A was part of a group of men which chased and attacked V and his friends with weapons including baseball bats, metal bars, and knives. V died from two deep knife wounds in his back. A was convicted for his part in the joint enterprise. The question for the House of Lords was whether to be guilty A had to foresee JV's intention or whether it could be fundamentally different from the act or acts which A foresaw as part of the joint enterprise.	Where A realises that JV might kill or intentionally inflict serious injury, but nevertheless continues to participate in the venture, that amounts to a sufficient mental element for A to be guilty of murder if JV, with the requisite intent, killed in the course of the venture, unless JV suddenly produced and used a weapon of which A knew nothing and which was more lethal than any weapon which A contemplated that JV or any other participant might be carrying and, for that reason, JV's act could be regarded as fundamentally different from anything foreseen by A.

⑨⑨ Key debates

Topic	'Joint enterprise'
Author/ Academic	Sir Richard Buxton
Viewpoint	Described by David Ormerod in the Commentary to *Yemoh* [2009] (on p 894) as 'a powerful and illuminating critique of the recent reform proposals and a defence of the common law'. (David Ormerod is a Law Commissioner.)
Source	[2009] Crim LR 233

Topic	'Being an accessory to one's own murder'
Author/ Academic	Sir Richard Buxton
Viewpoint	Examines the nature of accessorial liability in the context of the Supreme Court's decision in *Gnango* [2012].
Source	[2012] Crim LR 275

Topic	'Joint enterprise liability is dead: long live accessorial liability'
Author/ Academic	G Virgo
Viewpoint	A very helpful analysis of the language of accessorial and joint enterprise criminal liability through a critique of *Gnango* [2012].
Source	[2012] Crim LR 850

Problem question

On their release from prison for armed robbery, Kieran and Steve planned to get revenge on Dave who had informed on them to the police. They decided to pay a visit to his house one night, and to cause him grievous bodily harm.

Kieran and Steve asked a friend, Cooper, if he would act as a lookout. Cooper asked Kieran and Steve what they intended to do, and they told him that they were going to do a burglary. Cooper, who knew their reputation as violent criminals, agreed, provided that no weapons were used.

As they were breaking into the back window of Dave's house, Steve produced an iron bar. Cooper saw it and said 'Hey! No violence!' but Steve said 'Just in case.'

As they reached the first floor of Dave's house, he came out of his bedroom and shouted in alarm. Kieran lost his nerve and ran from the building. Steve, who hated Dave, hit him over the head with the iron bar six times intending to kill him. Dave died as a result.

When Steve got outside he was grabbed by a police officer because Cooper, who had become concerned, had called the police to let them know what was happening.

Steve has been convicted of murder.

Discuss the criminal liability, if any, of Kieran and Cooper.

An outline answer is included at the end of the book.

Exam questions

****

Essay question

There are more murderers who have killed without proof of intent to kill than who have killed with it.

Provide a critical analysis of this statement in respect of accessorial liability.

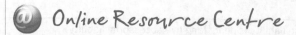 Online Resource Centre

To see an outline answer to this question log on to www.oxfordtextbooks.co.uk/orc/concentrate/

#11
Theft

- Theft is a technical and complex crime.
- There are five elements in theft:
  - Appropriation
  - Property
  - Belonging to another
  - Dishonesty
  - Intention permanently to deprive.
- The first three listed are the *actus reus* elements and the last two are the *mens rea*.
- The offence is under **s 1 Theft Act 1968**, but **ss 2–6** give (some) guidance on each of the elements.

Chapter overview

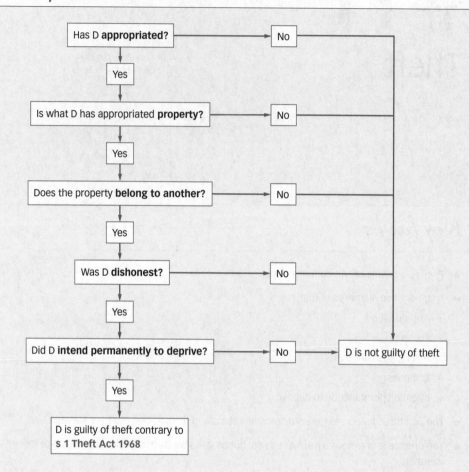

Introduction

Most people have a basic, and accurate, sense of what theft is. Examples of the most common forms of theft include shoplifting or picking someone's pocket, but they are not the only examples of conduct which can amount to theft. For example, it may even be theft if:

- the true owner *gives* the property to D;
- D *finds* the item;
- D *does not leave* the premises where he has taken the goods; or
- D *borrows* the item.

The offence of theft exists in order to give additional protection to existing civil property law rights. This would suggest, therefore, that the civil law and the criminal law would adopt the same definitions. We shall see, however, that decisions in the criminal courts have not adopted this approach, resulting in conflict between the criminal and the civil laws. There are five definitional elements in theft, and the prosecution bears the legal burden in respect of each of them. The offence is defined in **s 1 Theft Act 1968** which provides:

> A person is guilty of theft if he dishonestly appropriates property belonging to another with the intention of permanently depriving the other of it.

The five concepts used in the definition in s 1 are elaborated upon in the succeeding sections (ss 2–6). Table 11.1 will assist.

Table 11.1 The elements of theft

	Actus reus	*Mens rea*
Dishonestly		Section 2
Appropriates	Section 3	
Property	Section 4	
Belonging to another	Section 5	
Intention of permanently depriving		Section 6

Do not let the table mislead you. Theft is far more complex than learning five simple steps, because within those five elements are some technicalities which can trip students up.

Revision tip

We have to break the offence of theft into its five elements to learn them, but you should remember that *all elements must come together at a particular moment in time to constitute theft.*

We consider the *actus reus* before the *mens rea*.

Actus reus

Appropriation

The best way to tackle this element is to ask and answer a few fundamental questions.

What does the word 'appropriation' mean?

Section 3(1) Theft Act 1968 opens with the following words:

> Any assumption by a person of the rights of an owner amounts to an appropriation.

The 'rights of an owner' may include rights such as the right to sell property, hire it out, give it away, lend it, mortgage it, damage it, destroy it, or throw it away.

How many rights does D have to assume to appropriate?

This was answered in *Morris*[1984].

. . . .

Morris [1984] AC 320

D removed a price label from a joint of pork in a supermarket and attached it to a second, more expensive joint. The House of Lords held there was an appropriation when D switched the labels because D had adversely interfered with or usurped the rights of the owners of the goods to ensure that they were paid for at the proper price.

. . . .

In *Morris*, there were two parts to the House of Lords' decision:

- It is an appropriation to assume any one of the rights of the owner. *This is still good law and it answers the question above.*

- An appropriation takes place where D adversely interferes with an owner's right. There is, therefore, no appropriation if D does something he is allowed to do. *This is no longer good law* (it has since been held to be *obiter dicta*, but is not followed and could not even be said to be persuasive in light of recent decisions).

What if V allows D to assume that right?

Before the Theft Act 1968, the old definition of the offence of larceny required the prosecution to prove D took 'without the consent of the owner'. Therefore, if the owner permitted or allowed D to take the property, there was no offence. However, reference to consent was omitted from the Theft Act 1968.

Lawrence [1972] AC 626

V was an Italian student who hired a taxi in London. The taxi driver took £7 from V's open wallet (V obviously indicating for D to help himself to the amount of the fare) but the proper fare was only about 50 pence. D had committed theft. He had appropriated even though V had consented to D taking the money.

The House of Lords in *Gomez* [1993], which you will find in 'Key cases', p 146, approved the decision in *Lawrence* and held that the second part of the decision in *Morris* was *obiter dicta*. It is now the law that an adverse interference or usurpation is *not* necessary for there to be an appropriation.

✅ *Looking for extra marks?*

There is a very strong argument that *Gomez* [1993] should have been charged with obtaining by deception (an offence which has since been repealed) because there is no doubt he 'obtained' but considerable academic disagreement on whether he 'appropriated'. If you are asked an essay question which focuses on the meaning of appropriation, you might point out that had *Gomez* been charged with the correct crime, the law might have developed very differently.

A shopper appropriates property belonging to another as soon as he takes an article from the shelf. This applies to *honest* shoppers who intend to pay as much as to an intending shop-lifter; the former has of course committed only the *actus reus* and not the full offence of theft.

Revision tip

The result from *Lawrence* [1972] and *Gomez* [1993] is that there is nothing inherently wrong with 'appropriating' property. Only 'dishonest' appropriations can constitute the offence of theft.

What if V gives D the property?

If consent does not prevent an appropriation, is there an appropriation if V makes a valid gift of the property to D? A gift gives indefeasible (valid) ownership of the property.

Hinks [2001] 2 AC 241

This is the leading case. V, a middle-aged man of low IQ, inherited £60,000 on the death of his father who then gave it to D, who described herself as V's 'carer'. D claimed that the monies were fully valid gifts to her. The House of Lords held that the *Gomez* principle applied to the acquisition of a gift.

Actus reus

✳✳✳✳✳✳✳✳✳✳

For an analysis of the case, see 'Key debates', p 147. Virtually every acquisition of property now satisfies the *actus reus* of theft and therefore everything turns on dishonesty.

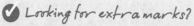 ✅ Looking for extra marks?

The extension of *Gomez* in *Hinks* is criticised because the purpose of the law of theft is to protect civil law property rights, yet the decision means a person can be convicted of stealing property which is, in the civil law, their own. Lord Steyn in *Hinks* rebutted this criticism.

Can D appropriate without physically touching the property?

The case of *Pitham and Hehl* (1976) suggests 'yes'.

....

Pitham and Hehl (1976) 65 Cr App R 45

V was sent to prison, leaving his house unoccupied. D introduced a prospective buyer to the house and invited him to buy V's furniture. The Court of Appeal held that D appropriated as soon as he invited the buyer to purchase.

....

How long does an appropriation last?

Because all five elements of theft have to occur at the same time this is an important question, as you will see from the outline answer at the end of the chapter.

....

Atakpu [1994] QB 69

Ds hired cars in Belgium and Germany using false passports. Ds drove the cars to England and were arrested on arrival. The Court of Appeal was open to the suggestion that appropriation can continue 'for as long as the thief can sensibly be regarded as in the act of stealing', but on the facts the cars were appropriated as soon as they were hired and the process of stealing had come to an end before they reached England.

....

Can the same property be appropriated by D a second time?

We looked only at the opening words of s 3(1) earlier, and it continues:

... and this includes, where he has come by the property (innocently or not) without stealing it, any later assumption of a right to it by keeping or dealing with it as owner.

This is sometimes referred to as the 'theft by finding' provision. D does not commit theft when he finds the property (he appropriates it but is honest) but may later be guilty of theft if he decides dishonestly to keep it (he appropriates it a second time).

Property

If the law does not recognise what is appropriated as property, there is no theft. **Section 4(1) Theft Act 1968** provides:

> 'Property' includes money and all other property, real or personal, including things in action and other intangible property.

It is not a great definition because it defines property by referring to all property, but it is so wide, it can safely be regarded as comprehensive. It does include property possession of which is illegal (*Smith* [2011]).

Money, real property, and personal property

Money means identifiable notes and coins, of any currency. Personal property usually means tangible items, such as jewellery, TV sets, vehicles, etc (and includes water and gas, but not electricity, information or corpses). Real property relates to land (but note the exceptions in s 4(2)).

Things in action and other intangible property

A thing in action (traditionally called a chose in action) is simply a right to sue. If X owes Y a debt, Y owns a thing in action; that is the right to sue X for the debt. All credit balances in bank accounts are debts, that is, the bank owes the account holder the sum represented by the amount of credit. A cheque is similar so that if V writes a cheque out to D, D owns a debt, and that is the right to have the bank pay him the amount of money on the cheque. The cheque, once written out with D's name, a payee, no longer belongs to V; and this is important for the next element of theft (belonging to another).

Belonging to another

The property must belong to another when it is appropriated, but it does not have to be stolen from the *legal* owner (*Smith* [2011]). **Section 5(1) Theft Act 1968** provides:

Property shall be regarded as belonging to any person having possession or control of it, or having in it any proprietary right or interest …

....

Turner (No 2) [1971] 1 WLR 901

D took his car to a garage to have it repaired. When the repairs were finished, the car was left in the road outside the garage. D drove the car away without paying for the repairs. This was theft because the garage proprietor was in possession or control of the car. Compare with *Meredith* [1973] where a different outcome was reached, but D did not owe money for any repairs.
....

Lost or abandoned?

A charge of theft will not fail simply because the true owner of the property cannot be identified, or because the property seems to have been lost or thrown away.

....

Hibbert v McKiernan [1948] 2 KB 142

D picked up lost golf balls from a golf club. This was theft. The golf club was in possession and control of the golf balls; the balls had not been abandoned (even if the legal owners had abandoned their search for them). In *Williams v Phillips* (1957), on the question of who owns property thrown into dustbins, the Divisional Court held the rubbish was in the possession of the householder and passed into the possession of the local authority when placed in the refuse lorries.
....

Cheques

We mentioned earlier that where V writes a cheque to D, the cheque (as a thing in action) no longer belongs to V, but to D. This means D cannot be convicted of theft of the cheque as a thing in action as it is not property belonging to another.

> ✅ *Looking for extra marks?*
>
> This short paragraph is a simplification of the more complex issues dealt with in *Preddy* [1996], an important case which also deals with electronic transfers of funds. You are advised to have a working knowledge of the decision.

D could be convicted of theft of the cheque as a piece of paper, but as that is so trivial, the CPS is unlikely to bring such a charge.

Issues where ownership passes to D when he appropriates

Ownership of certain property passes on delivery (s 18 Sale of Goods Act 1893, rule 5(2)). This includes meals in restaurants and petrol in vehicles, and is because the property cannot be returned. Therefore, does the property 'belong to another' when appropriated? The answer is yes. Is it theft? The answer is 'only if the *mens rea* is satisfied at the same time'.

Edwards v Ddin [1976] 1 WLR 942

D drove his car into a garage and requested the attendant to fill up the tank with petrol. After the attendant had done so, D drove off without paying. Unless the prosecution could prove D was dishonest at the moment of the appropriation, there could not be a theft. The ownership of the petrol had been transferred to D when the attendant put it into his car and it mixed with the petrol already there. This would now be an offence of making off without payment, which we examine in chapter 13.

D under obligation regarding the property and D getting the property by mistake

Sections 5(3) and 5(4) Theft Act 1968 provide that not all property in D's possession belongs to him for the purposes of theft. Section 5(3) provides:

> Where a person receives property from or on account of another, and is under an obligation to the other to retain and deal with that property or its proceeds in a particular way, the property or proceeds shall be regarded (as against him) as belonging to the other.

We do not have the space to go into detail here, but some of the cases illustrating this include:

- *Davidge v Bunnett* [1984], D spent the money her flatmates had given her to pay the gas bill on Christmas presents;
- *Hall* [1973], a travel agency was not under an obligation to use client money to pay for the client's specific holiday, the funds being paid into the business's general trading account; and
- *Wain* [1995], sponsorship money belongs to the trustees of the charity for which it was raised.

Section 5(4) provides:

> Where a person gets property by another's mistake, and is under an obligation to make restoration (in whole or in part) of the property or its proceeds or of the value thereof, then to the extent of that obligation the property or proceeds shall be regarded (as against him) as belonging to the person entitled to restoration …

This subsection covers the situation where D is overpaid by his employer. Although the salary overpayment is in D's control and possession, it belongs to the employer (see *AG's Ref (No 1 of 1983)* [1985]).

Mens rea

Dishonesty

> *Revision Tip*
>
> Always start by considering s 2(1) Theft Act 1968. Explain the subsections, apply them, and if they are not satisfied, move on to consider the case law (below).

Section 2 Theft Act 1968 does *not* define dishonesty. Section 2(1) simply states three situations in which D is *not* dishonest, if he appropriates property in the belief that:

(a) he has in law the right to deprive the other of it ... or

(b) he would have the other's consent if the other knew ... or

(c) the person to whom the property belongs cannot be discovered by taking reasonable steps.

All three subsections are phrased in terms of D's actual belief, so provided the jury is satisfied D did have that belief, he is not dishonest. Note that s 2(2) provides that D may be dishonest even if he is willing to pay for the property.

If D does not fall within s 2(1), and where dishonesty is an issue (ie contended between the parties) then the judge must direct the jury to answer the following question first:

- Was D dishonest according to the ordinary standards of reasonable and honest people?

If the jury answers that question 'no', then D is not guilty of theft. But if the jury answers that question 'yes', then a second question must be answered:

- Did D realise that what he was doing was by those standards dishonest?

These two questions are from the leading case on the meaning of dishonesty, *Ghosh* [1982] which you will find in 'Key cases', p 146.

Applying the test

> *Revision Tip*
>
> Lord Lane CJ, who gave the judgment in *Ghosh* [1982], gave a number of examples in his judgment where a person might be honest (acknowledging it is a jury matter, not a question of law). You will find it useful to read the judgment, looking out for:
> - the man who comes from a country where public transport is free,
> - Robin Hood, and
> - ardent anti-vivisectionists. →

→ As you read the judgment:
Do *you* think Robin Hood was dishonest according to the ordinary standards of reasonable and honest people?
If so, do you think *he knew* that reasonable and honest people would regard him as dishonest?

Is D dishonest if he appropriates a couple of pieces of paper from the stationery cupboard at work to write a shopping list? Because dishonesty is a question of fact for the jury (*Feely* [1973]), different juries will conclude differently. Some jurors may say it is dishonest, some jury members may say everyone does it so it can't be a crime. However, this could be a problem because the law has to be (relatively) certain so people can plan their conduct in light of whether that conduct is criminal or not. The *Ghosh* test may therefore be in breach of **Article 7 European Convention on Human Rights**, although a challenge to the uncertainty of the test did fail before the judge in *Pattni* [2001].

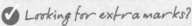 Looking for extra marks?

Research by Finch and Fafinski, summarised at www.thetimes.co.uk/tto/law/columnists/article2049324.ece, reveals serious misgivings about the way we view the question of dishonesty. The findings are useful for both essay and problem questions, and to raise your awareness about the *Ghosh* test.

Intention permanently to deprive

As you will realise quite quickly, you should avoid **s 6(1) Theft Act 1968** if at all possible. The best way to tackle this element of theft is to give the words ('intention of permanently depriving') their plain ordinary meaning (*Velumyl* [1989]). In most problem questions, it will usually be obvious, and it is only if your examiner uses words such as 'borrow' that you need to consider **s 6(1)**, which provides:

A person appropriating property belonging to another without meaning the other permanently to lose the thing itself is nevertheless to be regarded as having the intention of permanently depriving the other of it if his intention is to treat the thing as his own to dispose of regardless of the other's rights; and a borrowing or lending of it may amount to so treating it if, but only if, the borrowing or lending is for a period and in circumstances making it equivalent to an outright taking or disposal.

Revision tip

Be prepared to read the section a few times before you get a sense of it. The academic J Spencer has said that **s 6(1)** 'sprouts obscurities at every phrase' [1977] Crim LR 653.

Key cases

✱✱✱✱✱✱✱✱✱✱

Cases which illustrate the problems with the interpretation of s 6(1) include:

- *Lloyd* [1985], where borrowing films, even to make pirate copies, did not satisfy s 6(1) unless the intention was to return the thing in such a changed state that it had lost all its goodness or virtue.

- *DPP v Lavender* [1994], where D intended to treat the doors as his own, regardless of the council's rights when he took doors from a house being repaired to put on his girlfriend's house so as to replace damaged doors.

- *Fernandes* [1996], where a solicitor who used client money was held to have had intention permanently to deprive because in dealing with another's property for his own purpose, there was a risk of losing that property.

- *Cahill* [1993], where D moved a bundle of newspapers along a road, but there was no intention to 'dispose' of the papers so no theft.

- *Marshall* [1998], where selling unexpired London Underground tickets which would eventually be retained by the Underground was an intention permanently to deprive because it amounted to an intention to treat the tickets as D's own.

- *Vinall* [2012], where the Court of Appeal clarified that s 6(1) 'did not require that the thing had been disposed of, nor that the defendant intended to dispose of it in a particular way … [but whether D] exercised such a dominion over the property that it could be inferred that at the time of the taking he intended to treat the property as his own to dispose of regardless of the owner's rights'.

✱ Key cases

Case	Facts	Principle
Ghosh [1982] QB1053	D, a doctor, claimed fees for carrying out operations where either another surgeon had performed the operation or the operation had been carried out under the National Health Service.	It is no defence for a man to say, 'I knew that what I was doing is generally regarded as dishonest; but I do not regard it as dishonest myself. Therefore I am not guilty.' What he is, however, entitled to say is, 'I did not know that anybody would regard what I was doing as dishonest'.
Gomez [1993] AC 442	D, a shop assistant, persuaded the shop manager, V, to sell goods on the strength of cheques which D knew to be stolen.	An act authorised by the owner of goods constitutes an appropriation of goods, even if such consent had been obtained by deception.
Hinks [2001] 2 AC 241	V, a middle-aged man of low IQ, inherited £60,000 on the death of his father who then gave it to D, who described herself as V's 'carer'. D claimed that the monies were fully valid gifts to her.	The House of Lords held that the *Gomez* principle could apply to an indefeasible title to property where it was acquired by means of taking a gift from a person who was easily influenced. Therefore, there was an appropriation under the **Theft Act 1968**.

Key debates

Topic	'R v Hinks, case commentary'
Author/Academic	Professor Sir John Smith
Viewpoint	We cannot express it better than the author: 'The decision, with all respect, is contrary to common sense. It is absurd that a person should be guilty of stealing property which is his and in which no one else has any legal interest whatever.' For a contrary view, see S Shute, 'Appropriation and the law of theft' [2002] Crim LR 445.
Source	[2001] Crim LR 162 (the commentary is after the summary of the facts and the decision).

Topic	'Can dishonesty be salvaged? Theft and the grounding of the MSC Napoli'
Author/Academic	Richard Glover
Viewpoint	The author uses the example of people looting containers from a beach in 2007 to illustrate the test of dishonesty in theft.
Source	(2010) 74(1) J Crim L 53–76.

Exam questions

Problem question

The following separate events all took place on the same day, in the same supermarket.

1. Bert picked up a tin of salmon and put it in his pocket, intending to leave the store without paying for it. Thinking he might have been spotted by a store detective, however, he paid for the tin and left the store.

2. When Claire, a shopper, was loading the conveyor belt with the items from her trolley, she failed to notice a toothbrush and she left the store with it still in her trolley without having paid for it. Outside in the car park, she realised she had not paid for the toothbrush, but decided to keep it anyway.

3. Alex, who works on the cake counter, ate a cream cake after the store had closed. The cake was in a pile to be thrown away as it could not be offered for sale the next day. When his supervisor Denise saw him, she told him he should not eat the produce, he said, 'Fine, I'll pay for it then'.

Discuss the criminal liability, if any, for the offence of theft only, of Alex, Bert, and Claire.

An outline answer is included at the end of the book.

Exam questions

✳✳✳✳✳✳✳✳✳✳

Essay question

The problem with the offence of theft is that it can be committed even if the alleged thief assumes only one right of the owner, and even if the owner consents to the assumption of that right, and even if the alleged thief obtains indefeasible title to the property.

Discuss the validity of this statement.

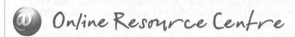

Online Resource Centre

To see an outline answer to this question log on to www.oxfordtextbooks.co.uk/orc/concentrate/

#12

Fraud

- There were eight offences under the **Theft Acts 1968** and **1978** which were based on deception.

- All eight deception offences have been abolished.

- The **Fraud Act 2006** replaced them with one offence of fraud and one offence of dishonestly obtaining services.

- The common law offence of conspiracy to defraud has not been abolished, but there have been sustained calls for it to be.

Chapter overview

D is guilty of fraud under s 1 Fraud Act 2006 if he:

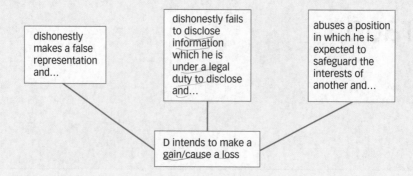

dishonestly makes a false representation and…

dishonestly fails to disclose information which he is under a legal duty to disclose and…

abuses a position in which he is expected to safeguard the interests of another and…

D intends to make a gain/cause a loss

D is guilty of an offence under s 11 Fraud Act 2006 if he dishonestly obtains services for himself or another where D intends not to pay (or not pay in full).

Introduction

Before the enactment of the Fraud Act 2006, there were eight offences that were broadly categorised as fraud, but were defined in terms of deception. The eight offences all involved dishonestly obtaining:

- property belonging to another by deception with intention permanently to deprive the other of it, contrary to s 15 Theft Act 1968 (TA 1968);
- a money transfer by deception, s 15A TA 1968;
- a pecuniary advantage by deception, s 16 TA 1968;
- a valuable security by deception, s 20(2) TA 1968;
- services by deception, contrary to s 1 Theft Act 1978 (TA 1978);
- the evasion of a liability by deception (three offences), s 2 TA 1978.

The Law Commission Report *Fraud* (Law Com No 276, 2002) criticised the deception offences and recommended their replacement with a fraud crime. This can be found in the Fraud Act 2006.

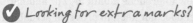

✅ *Looking for extra marks?*

Read the summary of the 2002 Report *Fraud,* particularly pp 13–22 for a summary of the criticisms of the Theft Acts 1968 and 1978 deception crimes.

Fraud

The offence of fraud is governed by the Fraud Act 2006. There is only one offence of fraud (s 1 Fraud Act 2006) with three ways of committing it, under ss 2–4. These are:

- by false representation,
- by failing to disclose information, and
- by abuse of position.

Fraud is a conduct crime (D lies), unlike the old deception offences which were result crimes (ie where D caused V to give him something by a deception), which means the prosecution does not have to prove causation. The new offence is potentially very wide indeed, a view made by David Ormerod (among others) (see 'Key debates', p 154).

Section 2, false representation

It is an offence if D dishonestly makes a false representation, and intends, by making the representation to make a gain for himself or another, or to cause loss to another or to expose another to a risk of loss. Under s 2(3) a representation is any representation as to fact or law, including a representation as to the state of mind of the maker or another person and it may be express or implied. The representation is false if it is either untrue or merely misleading. For example, the actions of *Lambie* in 'Key cases', p 154, would amount to a false (ie untrue) representation because D knew she did not have authority to pay with her credit card. However, what amounts to 'misleading' is undefined. A fraud can be committed against a machine, unlike under the previous law, because s 2(5) provides that:

> a representation may be regarded as made if it (or anything implying it) is submitted in any form to any system or device designed to receive, convey or respond to communications (with or without human intervention).

Revision tip

Learn the elements of s 2 and be aware of, for example, internet transactions where D uses a credit card which the credit company has told D should no longer be used.

The *mens rea* requirements are that the representation must be made dishonestly (*Ghosh* [1982]; s 2 Theft Act 1968 does not apply to the fraud crimes), knowing it is or it might be untrue or misleading, and it must be made with a view to produce a gain to D or another or loss or the risk of loss to the victim. The prosecution does not need to prove an actual gain or loss. Gain includes a gain by keeping what one has, as well as a gain by getting what one does not have, and loss includes a loss by not getting what one might get, as well as a loss by parting with what one has.

Section 3, failing to disclose

This is essentially a crime of lying by omission. The offence is committed where a person dishonestly fails to disclose to another person information which he is under a legal duty to disclose, and intends, by failing to disclose the information, to make a gain for himself or another, or to cause loss to another or to expose another to a risk of loss (s 3). The nature and extent of the legal duty is not defined in the Act, but is likely to encompass the facts of *Firth*, examined in 'Key cases', p 154.

Section 4, abuse of position

This method of committing fraud is worryingly broad. It covers any defendant who occupies a position in which he is expected to safeguard, or not to act against, the financial interests of another person, and where he dishonestly abuses that position, and intends, by means of the abuse of that position, to make a gain for himself or another, or to cause loss to another or to expose another to a risk of loss. The term 'abuse' is not defined. Nor is the concept of 'expectation' in terms of the interests of the other person, for example, whose expectation matters.

Dishonestly obtaining services

The offence of dishonestly obtaining services under s 11 Fraud Act 2006 parallels the offence of theft (see chapter 11) but it is phrased in terms of *obtaining services* rather than *appropriating property*. It is an offence to obtain services (neither 'obtain' nor 'services' is defined in the Act) for which a payment has been, is being, or will be expected, where D intends to avoid part payment or payment in full. There is an overlap with the fraud offence of making a false representation and the Crown Prosecution Service might prefer to bring a fraud charge because it is easier to prove (fraud is a conduct crime, and there is no need to prove that a specific thing (or a service) was obtained—which is needed under s 11).

Note that under s 11, the prosecution does not have to prove any deception or false representation.

Conspiracy to defraud

Conspiracy to defraud is a common law offence. It was described by the Law Commission in its 2002 report as 'an anomalous crime' because although it is a 'fraud' offence, D does not have to commit a deception, he does not have to cause economic loss through the carrying out of the agreement (*Wai Yu-tsang v R* [1992]), and it is not even necessary to prove that the conspirators' purpose was to defraud (provided they are aware that their agreement might result in fraud (*AG's Ref (No 1 of 1982)* [1983]). The crime consists of:

- an agreement,
- to deprive a person of something which is his, or
- to which he is or would be or might be entitled, or
- to injure some proprietary right of his.

In fact, this crime is so wide that it covers an agreement concerning conduct which, if carried out, does not consist in itself of a crime or even a tort.

....

Scott v MPC (1974) 3 All ER 1032

This is the leading case, where D entered into an agreement with employees of a cinema to lend him the films so that he could copy them and sell the pirate copies. He would then return the films, with the cinema owners none the wiser. The House of Lords acknowledged that a conspiracy to defraud does not have to involve the commission of a substantive offence and, on the facts, it could not be theft because D had no intention permanently to deprive (he always meant to give the property back). There was no deception because the owners were completely unaware of what was happening. However, there was an agreement, and it was to deprive the owners of the potential profits they would have made had people gone to the cinema to watch the films they would purchase instead from D. That is all that was needed for a conviction for conspiracy to defraud.

....

Key cases
****

There have been numerous calls for the abolition of this crime, but the Government refused to do so when the **Fraud Act 2006** was enacted. The reason given was that, if abolished, it could leave an unforeseen lacuna in the law.

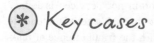 **Key cases**

Case	Facts	Principle
Firth (1990) 91 Cr App R 217	D was a consultant gynaecologist, and used a National Health Service hospital to treat a number of his private patients. He failed to tell the hospital that the patients were in fact private and the hospital did not charge either D or the patients for the use of the facilities.	The offence of dishonestly obtaining exemption or abatement of liability by deception could be committed by an act of commission or one of omission. This conduct would probably now be a fraud offence by breach of (at least) **s 3 Fraud Act 2006** (possibly by **s 4** as well).
Lambie [1982] AC 449	D had exceeded the limit on her credit card and agreed to return the card to the bank. However, she used it to make another purchase in a shop.	The House of Lords held that the presentation of the credit card had been a representation of D's authority to make a contract on the bank's behalf. It was false, and it was open to the jury to find that the manager had been induced by D's representation.
Scott v MPC [1974] 3 All ER 1032	The defendant had an agreement with employees of a cinema to lend him the films so that he could copy them and sell the pirate copies. He would then return the films, with the cinema owners none the wiser.	The offence of conspiracy to defraud is complete where the intention is to cause the victim economic loss by dishonest means. Deceit is not an essential ingredient of the offence.

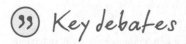 **Key debates**

Topic	'The Fraud Act 2006—criminalising lying'
Author/Academic	David Ormerod
Viewpoint	The **Fraud Act 2006** is welcome, but too broad, undefined, and possibly unworkable.
Source	[2007] Crim LR 193

Topic	'The Fraud Act 2006—some early observations and comparisons with the former law'
Author/Academic	Carol Withey
Viewpoint	Assesses the extent to which the new offences address the problems in connection with the former deception offences.
Source	(2007) 71(3) J Crim L 220

 Exam questions

Problem question

Stacey was a plastic surgeon who did operations for both National Health Service patients (who do not have to pay) and private (paying) patients. She did all of the operations at the local National Health Service hospital on the understanding that she would always declare which patients were private, and they would be invoiced by the hospital separately.

Stacey carried out eight private operations. She did not declare to the hospital that these patients were private. She sent the patients invoices for their operations, which they all paid directly to her. Stacey did not pass on their payments to the hospital. The hospital administrators listed the patients as National Health Service patients because they had not been told to the contrary. The payments came to a total of over £10,000.

Stacey was also authorised to place orders over the internet for medical supplies using the hospital's credit card. Stacey placed a number of orders online for personal items, and paid using the hospital's credit card.

Consider Stacey's criminal liability, if any, for offences under the Fraud Act 2006.

An outline answer is included at the end of the book.

Essay question

The effect of the Fraud Act 2006 is to criminalise lying.

Critically evaluate the truth of this statement.

 Online Resource Centre

To see an outline answer to this question log on to www.oxfordtextbooks.co.uk/orc/concentrate/

#13

Other property offences

Key facts

- There are six offences examined in this chapter:
    - Criminal damage
    - Robbery
    - Burglary
    - Handling stolen goods
    - Making off and
    - Squatting.
- What the offences share is that they relate in some way to property.
- Rarely examined on their own, these topics are often assessed as part of bigger questions, sometimes incorporating other offences (eg theft, assault) and sometimes involving aspects of the general defences too.

Chapter overview

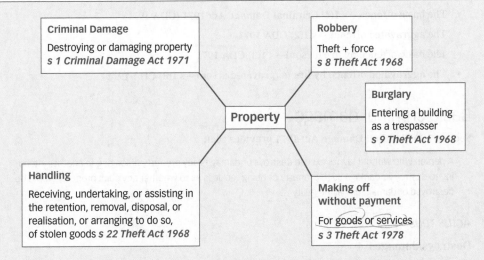

Criminal Damage

Destroying or damaging property
s 1 Criminal Damage Act 1971

Robbery

Theft + force
s 8 Theft Act 1968

Burglary

Entering a building
as a trespasser
s 9 Theft Act 1968

Property

Handling

Receiving, undertaking, or assisting in
the retention, removal, disposal, or
realisation, or arranging to do so,
of stolen goods *s 22 Theft Act 1968*

**Making off
without payment**

For goods or services
s 3 Theft Act 1978

Criminal damage

There are four ways of committing criminal damage:

- The basic offence—s 1(1) Criminal Damage Act 1971 (CDA 1971)
- The aggravated offence—s 1(2) CDA 1971
- The basic offence by fire (arson)—s 1(3) CDA 1971
- The aggravated offence by fire (aggravated arson)—s 1(3) CDA 1971.

Basic criminal damage

Section 1(1) Criminal Damage Act 1971 provides that:

A person who without lawful excuse destroys or damages any property belonging to another intending to destroy or damage such property or being reckless as to whether any such property would be destroyed or damaged shall be guilty …

Actus reus

Destroys/damages

Whether property is destroyed or damaged is a question of fact and degree. 'Destroy' indicates finality, eg demolishing a building or crushing a car. 'Damage' can be temporary or permanent but must involve physical harm or impairment of the value or utility of the property.

Hardman v CC Avon [1986] Crim LR 330

Daubing the pavement with water-based paint, which was easily washed off, *was* damage because it took time and expense to do so. However, in *A v R* [1978], spitting on a police officer's coat was *not* damage because the coat was restored simply by wiping it off. The value and utility of the coat was not affected.

Any property belonging to another

Broadly speaking, these offences replicate the provisions relating to theft (see s 10 CDA 1971).

Without lawful excuse

As well as general defences (see chapters 14 and 15) the CDA 1971 provides two specific defences of lawful excuse (which are not available for the aggravated offence under s 1(2)). Section 5(2) CDA 1971 provides that a person has a lawful excuse:

(a) if … he believed that the person … whom he believed to be entitled to consent to the destruction of or damage to the property in question had so consented, or would have consented to it if he or they had known of the destruction or damage and its circumstances; or,

(b) if he destroyed or damaged ... the property in question ... in order to protect property belonging to himself or another ... and he believed—

(i) that the property ... was in immediate need of protection; and

(ii) that the means of protection adopted ... were ... reasonable having regard to all the circumstances.

Jaggard v Dickinson [1981] QB 527

D broke two windows and damaged a curtain in V's house because D, due to voluntary intoxication, mistakenly believed that she was damaging the property of X, a friend, and that he (X) would have consented to her doing so. The Divisional Court held that it was clear from s 5(2)(a) that if the belief was honestly held it was irrelevant that it was unreasonable. See also 'Mistake' in chapter 14, p 181.

Despite the apparently subjective wording of s 5(2)(b), there is an objective element.

Hill and Hall (1989) 89 Cr App R 74

The Court of Appeal held that the test was whether, on the facts believed by D (subjective), the damage could amount to something done to protect her home and that of her nearby friends (the objective test). See also *Hunt* (1978).

Mens rea

Revision tip

Do not state the *mens rea* is 'intention or recklessness'. There are two elements to the *mens rea* and you must be specific when describing them.

The prosecution must prove D intended or was reckless as to *the damage/destruction and* that D knew or believed that the *property belonged to another*. In *Smith* [1974], D (the tenant) did not *intend* to damage property *belonging to another* (the landlord) because he thought the property was his own. Recklessness is assessed subjectively: *R v G* [2004], see 'Key cases', p 166 and 'Key debates', p 166.

Aggravated criminal damage

Section 1(2) CDA contains the aggravated form of criminal damage, and it provides:

A person who without lawful excuse destroys or damages any property, whether belonging to himself or another—

(a) intending to destroy or damage any property or being reckless as to whether any property would be destroyed or damaged; and

(b) intending by the destruction or damage to endanger the life of another or being reckless as to whether the life of another would be thereby endangered; shall be guilty …

The leading case on s 1(2) is *Steer* [1988], which you will find in 'Key cases', p 166. Many of the terms are duplicated from s 1(1) and carry the same meaning, but there are two important differences:

1. the property need not belong to another, and

2. the lawful excuse defence under s 5 does not apply to the s 1(2) offence.

Revision tip

There are four ways of charging the offence in respect of the *mens rea*. If you have a problem question and you are told the wording of the charge, it is important you check its *exact* wording (see eg *Wenton* (2012)). Misreading this could cause confusion and lose marks.

The four ways of charging the offence of aggravated criminal damage are set out in Table 13.1.

Table 13.1 Aggravated Criminal Damage

1	*Actus reus*	+	Intention to destroy or damage any property	+	Intention by the destruction or damage to endanger the life of another
2	*Actus reus*	+	Intention to destroy or damage any property	+	Reckless as to whether the life of another would be endangered by the destruction or damage
3	*Actus reus*	+	Reckless as to whether property would be destroyed or damaged	+	Intention by the destruction or damage to endanger the life of another
4	*Actus reus*	+	Reckless as to whether property would be destroyed or damaged	+	Reckless as to whether the life of another would be endangered by the destruction or damage

Careful attention to these will assist you to grasp the *mens rea* elements in the conjoined appeals *Webster and Warwick*.

Webster and Warwick [1995] 2 All ER 168

Webster: D pushed a stone off a railway bridge which penetrated the roof of a train. D was convicted of causing damage with intent to endanger life. The Court of Appeal substituted a conviction of damaging property *being reckless* as to whether life was endangered. Whilst D had intended that the stone should crash through the roof, he was only *reckless* to the danger that the *damage* would cause.

Warwick: D drove a stolen car and threw bricks at a pursuing police car, smashing its rear window. D was convicted of causing damage with intent to endanger life and his conviction was upheld. D's intentional breaking of the window allowed the jury to infer an intention to shower V with broken glass, causing him to lose control of his vehicle, and such damage was capable of endangering life.

Arson

Where either s 1(1) or s 1(2) is committed by fire, the charge is arson, eg D is charged with committing criminal damage contrary to s 1(1) and s 1(3).

Robbery

Section 8 Theft Act 1968 provides:

A person is guilty of robbery if he steals, and immediately before, or at the time of doing so, and in order to do so, he uses force on any person or puts or seeks to put any person in fear of being there and then subjected to force.

Actus reus

Robbery is theft *plus*. It is an aggravated form of theft, so no theft; no robbery (see *Robinson* [1977], p 162).

Force or threat of force

The word 'force' is not defined in the **Theft Act 1968**, but it is not a complicated word and is a question of fact for the jury. In *Dawson* (1977) a nudge amounted to force, but in *P v DPP* [2012], snatching a cigarette from V without direct physical contact with V was not. That said, force itself need not be used; if D threatens V with force, that too is robbery.

Immediately before or at the time of ... and in order to

Again, this is a question of fact for the jury.

Hale (1979) 68 Cr App R 415

D1 tied V up in the kitchen and D2 went upstairs to steal jewellery. The jury was satisfied that the force used by D1 enabled D2 to steal, so both committed robbery.

Mens rea

Because proof of theft is a prerequisite for conviction for robbery, the *mens rea* of theft must be proved (which is why, in *Robinson*, there was no robbery), but there is no *mens rea* as to the force element.

Robinson [1977] Crim LR 173

D threatened V, who owed D a substantial amount of money, with a knife. D believed he had the right in law to the money, but he knew he should not threaten V in this way. Because **s 2 Theft Act 1968** (see 'Dishonesty' in chapter 11, p 144) provided that D was not dishonest, there was no theft, and therefore no robbery.

Burglary

This offence is governed by **s 9 Theft Act 1968**, which provides:

(1) A person is guilty of burglary if—
    (a) he enters any building or part of a building as a trespasser and with intent to commit any such offence as is mentioned in subsection (2) below; or
    (b) having entered any building or part of a building as a trespasser he steals or attempts to steal anything in the building or part of it or inflicts or attempts to inflict on any person therein any grievous bodily harm.
(2) The offences referred to in subsection (1)(a) above are offences of stealing anything in the building or part of in question, of inflicting on any person therein any grievous bodily harm … and of doing unlawful damage to the building or anything therein.

Section 9 creates two offences:

- **s 9(1)(a)**—D is guilty on entry to a building or part of it as a trespasser if he intends to steal, inflict GBH, or cause criminal damage, and
- **s 9(1)(b)**—having entered a building or part of it as a trespasser, D is guilty if he then commits theft or GBH or attempts to do so.

Actus reus

Entry

This is not the same as 'breaking and entering' (which does not exist as an offence) and D's whole body need not be in the building for there to be an entry. What amounts to an entry is a question of fact for the jury. In *Brown* [1985], D kept his feet on the ground and leaned through a broken window into a shop to rummage through the goods. This was an 'effective' entry. In *Ryan* [1996], D had entered when only his head and right arm were in the building.

As a trespasser

The law requires D to know he is a trespasser or be reckless to that fact.

Collins [1973] QB 100

D, who was naked except for his socks, climbed a ladder to the window of a girl's bedroom, intending to have sexual intercourse by force if need be (intention to rape was an ulterior offence in s 9(2) at that time). He was climbing through the window when the girl, who had been drinking alcohol, noticed him, and invited him in for sexual intercourse, mistaking him for her boyfriend. The critical question was *when* the girl's permission to enter her room was given, before or after he had entered the room. If he was outside when the permission was granted, he would not have entered as a trespasser.

A person who has permission to enter the building, but exceeds that permission, becomes a trespasser:

Jones and Smith [1976] 1 WLR 672

The two defendants entered Smith's father's house and stole television sets. For the purposes of s 9(1)(b) Theft Act 1968 a person was a trespasser if he entered the premises of another knowing that, or being reckless whether, he was entering in excess of any permission that had been given to him to enter.

✅ *Looking for extra marks?*

The reasoning behind the decisions in *Collins* [1973] and *Jones and Smith* [1976] differs. Collins was always going to exceed V's permission to enter her room, as he was harbouring an intention to have sexual intercourse by force. It seems the criminal law has not clearly settled when a person is a trespasser and when he is not.

Any building or part of

The word 'building' is not defined, but probably requires some sort of permanence, so probably does not include a tent. 'Part of' a building includes areas separated off, including the area behind a till in a shop (*Walkington* (1979)).

Mens rea

D must know or realise he is a trespasser. For an offence under s 9(1)(a), the prosecution must prove D had the necessary intent *on entry*.

....

AG's Refs (Nos 1 and 2 of 1979) [1980] QB 180

D entered a building as a trespasser with intent to steal, but the building was empty. The Court of Appeal held it is not necessary to specify any particular article as being the object of D's intention, nor is it a defence that D intended to steal only if he found something worth stealing.

....

For an offence under s 9(1)(b), the prosecution must prove D formed the *mens rea* of the ulterior offence.

Handling stolen goods

Section 22(1) Theft Act 1968 provides:

A person handles stolen goods if (otherwise than in the course of the stealing) knowing or believing them to be stolen goods he dishonestly receives the goods, or dishonestly undertakes or assists in their retention, removal, disposal or realisation by or for the benefit of another person, or if he arranges to do so.

Actus reus

There are 18 ways of carrying out the *actus reus*: *receiving* (1); *undertaking* retention, removal, disposal, or realisation by or for the benefit of another person (4); *assisting in* retention, removal, disposal, or realisation by or for the benefit of another person (4); arranging to do any of these (9).

Revision tip

It is not always necessary to handle for the benefit of another. To which method of handling does this apply? See *Bloxham* [1983]. Be very careful of this point when answering problem questions and make sure you check who the handling is benefiting.

Mens rea

The prosecution must prove D was dishonest (*Ghosh* [1982]) *and* knew or believed the goods to be stolen (*Hall* (1985)), suspicion is not enough (*Moys* (1984)).

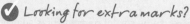 *Looking for extra marks?*

One of the complexities in this offence relates to the *proceeds* of the handled goods (s 24(2)). If this is a topic on which you are likely to be assessed, refer to a leading textbook.

Making off without payment

Also known as bilking, this is the offence of leaving without paying.

Section 3 Theft Act 1978 provides:

A person who, knowing that a payment on the spot for any goods supplied or service done is required or expected from him, dishonestly makes off without having paid as required or expected and with intent to avoid payment of the amount due shall be guilty ...

Actus reus

- Making off means departing or disappearing (*Brooks and Brooks* (1983))
- on the spot
- without having paid as required or expected
- for goods supplied or services done.

Troughton v MPC [1987] Crim LR 138

D was so drunk he could not tell the taxi driver where he lived, except for saying it was '... somewhere in Highbury'. The taxi driver got to Highbury but could still not get any sense out of D. D tried to leave the car, so the taxi driver drove D to a police station. D could not be guilty of making off because the time that payment would have been due had not been reached.

Vincent [2001] 1 WLR 1172

D stayed in a hotel for some weeks and left without paying. D said he had an agreement with hotel owners (Vs) that he would not pay because he was owed money for work he had done. Vs said they had been conned into that agreement, but any deception was irrelevant. An agreement had existed and there was therefore no expectation that D would pay.

Mens rea

D must:

- act dishonestly (*Ghosh* [1982]) at the time of making off;
- know that payment on the spot is required or expected of him (*Brooks and Brooks* (1983)); and
- intend to avoid payment of the amount due (*Allen* [1985]). D must intend never to pay; if he intends to pay at a later date, he does not satisfy the *mens rea*.

Squatting

Section 144 Legal Aid, Sentencing and Punishment of Offenders Act 2012 creates an offence of squatting in a residential building. The crime was created in response to public concern about the harm trespassers cause by entering and then staying and living in someone else's property.

 **Key cases**

Case	Facts	Principle
R v G [2004] 1 AC 1034	Two boys, aged 11 and 12, set fire to newspapers in the yard at the back of a shop and threw the lit newspapers under a wheelie bin. They left the yard without putting out the fire. The burning newspapers set fire to the bin, spread to the shop, and caused £1m damage. They expected the newspapers to burn themselves out on the concrete floor of the yard and it was accepted that neither of them appreciated the risk of the fire spreading in the way that it did. The trial judge had directed the jury in accordance with the objective test given in *Caldwell*.	Overruling *Caldwell*, the House of Lords held a person acts recklessly within the meaning of **s 1 CDA 1971** in respect of a result when he is aware of a risk that it will occur, and it is, in the circumstances known to him, unreasonable to take that risk.
Steer [1988] AC 111	After a disagreement with his business partner, D went to his partner's house and fired shots from a rifle at two windows and the door. No injuries were caused. D was charged with damaging property with intent, being reckless as to whether life would be endangered, contrary to **s 1(2)** of the **1971 Act**.	Intention or recklessness in **s 1(2)** is directed to danger to life caused by the *damaged property* and not by the *way* in which it is damaged.

Key debates

Topic	The meaning of recklessness in the criminal law and whether it should contain an objective element
Author/Academic	Dori Kimel
Viewpoint	Provides a detailed analysis of the decision in *Caldwell*, its effects (in eg *Elliott*) and the decision of the House of Lords to overrule it in *R v G*.
Source	'Inadvertent recklessness in criminal law' [2004] LQR 548

Topic	'Banksy's graffiti: a not-so-simple case of criminal damage'
Author/Academic	Ian Edwards
Viewpoint	The author takes the reader through the *actus reus* and *mens rea* elements of criminal damage and applies them (or not) to the case of a graffiti artist.
Source	(2009) 73(4) J Crim L 345

 **Exam questions**

Problem question

Lenny used to be employed as a butler by Noble. Noble sacked Lenny a few weeks ago over a dispute about unpaid wages. Lenny knew that Noble was planning a holiday abroad. Lenny asked Morris, a chef in Noble's house, to disable the alarm system whilst Noble was on holiday. Morris agreed to do as Lenny asked.

On the first night of Noble's holiday, Lenny broke into Noble's house meaning to open Noble's safe and take the money Lenny believed he was owed. Morris had disabled the house alarm, but Noble had changed the safe combination and Lenny could not open the safe.

As Lenny left the house, he saw a painting he knew to be worth about the same amount he thought he was owed. He took the painting and left.

Assess the criminal liability, if any, of Lenny and Morris.

An outline answer is included at the end of the book.

#14
Defences I

Key facts

- In this chapter we examine age, insanity, automatism, intoxication, and mistake.

- If D is under the age of ten, he is deemed incapable of criminal liability.

- Insanity is where D proves he had a disease of mind which caused a defect of reason so that D did not know the nature and quality of his act or that it was wrong. If the disease of mind was due solely to an external cause, the defence is non-insane automatism rather than insanity.

- Non-insane automatism is an assertion by D that the prosecution cannot prove the *actus reus* of the offence because D was not in control of his muscular movements. D has to raise evidence of this and the prosecution has to disprove it.

- Intoxication rarely succeeds as a defence. Involuntary intoxication is a defence if D does not form *mens rea*. Voluntary intoxication is a defence only if D is charged with a specific intent crime and D did not form *mens rea*. If D is charged with a basic intent crime, voluntary intoxication is only a defence if D would not have formed *mens rea* when sober.

- Mistake is a defence provided the mistake prevents D forming *mens rea*.

- As you can see from this list, most defences are actually negative assertions, which means that D is alleging the prosecution cannot prove a definitional element of the offence (*actus reus* or *mens rea*).

- The burden of disproof in relation to the defences usually lies on the prosecution.

Chapter overview

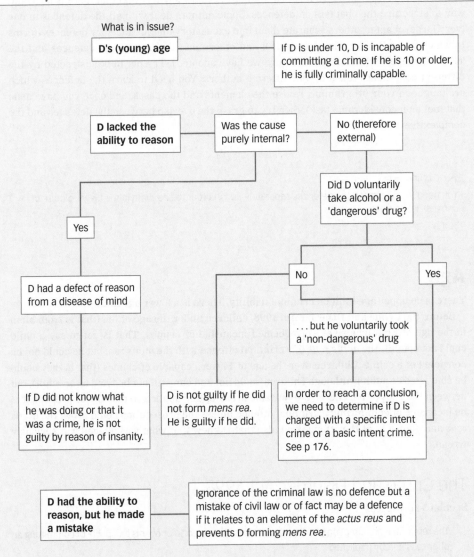

What is in issue?

D's (young) age — If D is under 10, D is incapable of committing a crime. If he is 10 or older, he is fully criminally capable.

D lacked the ability to reason — Was the cause purely internal? — No (therefore external)

Did D voluntarily take alcohol or a 'dangerous' drug?

Yes

D had a defect of reason from a disease of mind

No

Yes

... but he voluntarily took a 'non-dangerous' drug

If D did not know what he was doing or that it was a crime, he is not guilty by reason of insanity.

D is not guilty if he did not form *mens rea*. He is guilty if he did.

In order to reach a conclusion, we need to determine if D is charged with a specific intent crime or a basic intent crime. See p 176.

D had the ability to reason, but he made a mistake — Ignorance of the criminal law is no defence but a mistake of civil law or of fact may be a defence if it relates to an element of the *actus reus* and prevents D forming *mens rea*.

Introduction

A quick comparison of the leading criminal law textbooks will reveal that there is no 'right' way to structure the chapters on defences. Some authors deal with all the defences in one (very large) chapter; others separate them into excusatory and justificatory defences (terms to which we will return in chapter 15); and others into the 'reasoning' defences and the 'other' defences (which is the structure we have adopted). Try not to be distracted by the different approaches taken by the different authors. You need to learn the defences which are taught on your programme, revise the elements and the cases, and once you have done that (not an inconsiderable task), then try to grasp the overlap between the defences and the complexities within them.

Revision tip

You need to understand the defences separately first in order to see them in the bigger picture of criminal liability later.

Age

There is no upper age limit on criminal liability. There is a lower age limit.

Before the **Crime and Disorder Act 1998**, children under the age of ten (that is from birth to the age of nine inclusive) were deemed incapable of crimes. That is not to say a child could not commit the *actus reus* of a criminal offence with the *mens rea*, but he could not be convicted of a crime. Children over the age of 14 were capable of crimes (that is they could be convicted as adults, although children could not and can still not be tried as an adult), but between the ages of ten and 14, a rebuttable presumption applied so that D was presumed to be incapable of committing a criminal offence unless the prosecution could prove the *actus reus* and *mens rea* of the offence *and also* that D knew that what was alleged was seriously wrong.

The Crime and Disorder Act 1998

Section 34 provides:

> The rebuttable presumption of criminal law that a child aged 10 or over is incapable of committing an offence is hereby abolished.

The effect of the section was unclear until *R v T* [2008]. Did it mean all children aged ten to 14 were fully criminally capable? Or did it remove the rebuttable presumption so that D was capable unless he raised his capacity as an issue? (See the arguments made each way in *CPS v P* [2008].) In *R v T* it was the first question which was answered affirmatively.

....

R v T [2008] EWCA Crim 815

D was aged 12 at the time of committing offences of inciting a child under 13 years of age to engage in sexual activity. There was no dispute that he had committed the offences. The only question was whether D was entitled to raise the issue of his capacity to know that those acts were wrong. The Court of Appeal held that he could not.

....

The law today

Aged birth to nine inclusive: not capable of criminal liability.

Aged ten and over: capable of criminal liability and D cannot argue he was too young to have capacity.

Insanity

Revision tip

Insanity at the time of trial is dealt with differently from insanity at the time of the commission of the offence. If D is insane at the time of the trial, it is dealt with as unfitness to plead, and you are referred to **s 4 Criminal Procedure (Insanity) Act 1964** and related case law, including *Antoine* [2001].

Insanity as a defence may also be referred to as **insane automatism**. There is certainly an overlap between insane automatism and non-insane automatism (referred to here as simply insanity and automatism respectively) to which we will return. Insanity is a reasonably straightforward defence to learn, but it is controversial in its effect. The single most important thing to realise at the start is that insanity is a legal defence and not a description of a medical condition.

The elements of the defence

The leading case is *M'Naghten* (1843) (which is also reported with the spelling McNaughten, McNaghten, or McNaughton. Do not allow yourself to worry about the different spellings).

....

M'Naghten's case (1843) 8 ER 718

D was suffering from morbid delusions and a persecution syndrome. He fired his gun at the Prime Minister's secretary, believing he was actually shooting the Prime Minister, because M'Naghten believed there was a plot against him. The House of Lords stated:

> the jury should be directed that every man is presumed to be sane ... until the contrary be proved to their satisfaction, and that to establish a defence on the ground of insanity it must

be clearly proved that at the time of committing the act the party accused was labouring under such a defect of reason, from disease of the mind, as not to know the nature and quality of the act he was doing, or, if he did know it, that he did not know that he was doing what was wrong.

So we can see there are four elements to the defence, but only three have to be proved (and proved by D on a balance of probabilities):

Either defect of reason + disease of mind + D did not know the nature and quality of his act

Or defect of reason + disease of mind + D did know the nature and quality of his act BUT did not know what he was doing was wrong.

Defect of reason

This element means D must prove he was deprived of the power of reasoning.

Clarke [1972] 1 All ER 219

D was charged with shoplifting. She admitted taking the goods but said that it was due to absent-mindedness and depression. On appeal, it was decided that this was not a defect of reason.

Disease of mind

This is by far the most significant element to the defence.

Revision tip

Structure your revision into three parts. First, learn the definition of disease of mind from *Sullivan* [1984] immediately below. Secondly, learn the cases which illustrate the element. Thirdly, identify that because of the definition, certain 'diseases' do *not* fall within the defence of insanity which perhaps should (eg mental diseases) and some *do* which perhaps should not (eg epilepsy).

The authority for the definition of disease of mind is *Sullivan* [1984], which you will find in 'Key cases' on p 184. The House of Lords expressly stated that the word 'mind' in the *M'Naghten Rules* is used in the ordinary sense of the *mental faculties of reason, memory, and understanding,* but a disease of mind cannot arise from an external cause. Therefore, for there to be a disease of mind, there has to be an internal cause of the defect of reason:

- *Sullivan* [1984]: epilepsy was a disease of mind;
- *Kemp* [1957]: D was charged with causing GBH to his wife. He suffered from arterio-sclerosis (the hardening of the arteries) which led to a congestion of blood in the brain (a well-recognised consequence of the disease) causing a temporary lapse of consciousness in which state the attack was made; and
- *Burgess* [1991]: although D argued that sleepwalking fell into the defence of non-insane automatism, below, the Court of Appeal considered *Sullivan* and concluded that

sleepwalking is due to an internal disorder and where it manifests itself in violence and might recur (see *Bratty* [1963]) that is a disease of mind and D is insane.

So, if the defect of reason arises from an external cause, it cannot be a disease of mind, and it is not insanity. What then is it? It is (non-insane) automatism. The best way to grasp the difference between internal and external causes is to contrast two cases; *Quick* [1973] and *Hennessey* [1989].

Quick [1973] QB 910

D was a nurse who was charged with assaulting a patient. D, a diabetic, gave evidence that he had taken insulin as prescribed on the morning of the assault, had then drunk alcohol and eaten little food and had no recollection of the assault. He called medical evidence to the effect that he was suffering hypoglycaemia. The Court of Appeal held that 'disease of the mind' was a malfunctioning of the mind caused by disease. It did not include the application to the body of some external factor, such as insulin.

Hennessey [1989] 1 WLR 287

In this case, D was also an insulin-dependent diabetic who *had not* taken insulin and had not eaten for several days. He sought to raise a defence of automatism, in that the offences with which he was charged were committed during a state of hyperglycaemia. That, said the courts, was an internal cause (the diabetes itself) and not an external cause (the insulin).

Revision tip

The physical effects of hypoglycaemia and hyperglycaemia are similar, yet the effects in law are very different. Refer to any standard criminal law textbook for criticism of these cases.

Does not know what he is physically doing

In essence the court is asking whether D appreciated what he was physically doing and what the physical consequences of his conduct were.

Revision tip

Many textbooks provide colourful examples of this element, including cutting off a sleeping person's head to see him look for it when he wakes up. Make sure you can recite and apply at least one example.

Or does not know it is against the law

This is best illustrated by the following very sad case:

Windle [1952] 2 QB 82

D was a man of 40 years of age, of little resolution, and weak character who suffered from a form of communicated insanity. He was in an unhappy marriage with a woman 18 years his senior who had very serious depression. D killed his wife by giving her 100 aspirins. On arrest, he said 'I suppose they will hang me for this?' Unfortunately, and despite a defect of reason and a disease of mind, he knew physically what he was doing and he obviously knew it was 'wrong' (contrary to law).

Operation of the defence

Insanity is a general defence and can be pleaded to all crimes. Procedurally, the prosecution must first prove that D performed the *actus reus* of the offence alleged (s 2(1) Trial of Lunatics Act 1883). If the prosecution cannot prove the *actus reus*, D must be acquitted, but the prosecution does not have to prove that the defect of reason prevented D having the *mens rea* for the offence charged.

The burden of proving the defence itself lies on D, and he must prove it on a balance of probability. The law requires D to adduce evidence from two or more registered medical practitioners, at least one of whom is approved to give such evidence (s 1 Criminal Procedure (Insanity and Unfitness to Plead) Act 1991). On the allocation of the burden of proof to D, see the 'Looking for extra marks?' box in chapter 7, p 90.

If D does prove he was insane at the time of the crime, he is found not guilty by reason of insanity (also called the 'special verdict'), and he will be made the subject of a disposal order, including (but not limited to) hospital and supervision orders under the Mental Health Act 1983.

It was once the case that a defendant found not guilty by reason of insanity to murder was subject to an indefinite period of detention in a secure mental hospital, but this was changed by the Domestic Violence, Crime and Victims Act 2004.

What is the difference between insanity and diminished responsibility?

Once you have revised the individual defences, you need to appreciate that there is overlap between them. For example, it is not unusual for an examiner to set a question where D has killed, but was suffering some inability to reason at the time. This gives the candidate scope to discuss a number of defences (subject to what is relevant to the facts of the question) including insanity, diminished responsibility, loss of self-control, automatism, and perhaps intoxication too.

Table 14.1 is designed with two purposes: (a) to show you how insanity and diminished responsibility compare; and (b) to give you an idea on how to structure a comparison chart which you can use when you are revising the similarities and differences between any of the other defences listed previously. You should draw out the grid in Table 14.1 and annotate it with cases.

Table 14.1 Comparing diminished responsibility and insanity

	Diminished responsibility	Insanity
Source of law	Section 2 Homicide Act 1957 as amended	*M'Naghten's case* (1843)
Burden of proof	Defendant on a balance of probabilities	Defendant on a balance of probabilities
Availability	Murder only	All crimes
Effect	Reduces murder to voluntary manslaughter	Not guilty by reason of insanity
Elements	Abnormality of mental functioning which explains D's acts	Disease of mind
	Recognised mental condition	Defect of reason
	Substantial impairment of ability	Did not know nature and quality/did not know it was wrong

Automatism

We continue to examine cases where D has a defence based on his inability to reason.

What does 'automatism' mean?

In *Bratty v AG for N Ireland* [1963], Lord Denning stated that automatism means:

> an act which is done by the muscles without any control by the mind, such as a spasm, a reflex action or a convulsion; or an act done by a person who is not conscious of what he is doing, such as an act done whilst suffering from concussion …

Essentially, what is required is that the defendant's mind has no control over his limbs:

....

Broome v Perkins (1987) 85 Cr App R 321

D was a diabetic who suffered a hypoglycaemic attack whist driving home. He was able to negotiate road junctions and traffic lights and he veered away from other vehicles. D was charged with driving without due care and attention. Although hypoglycaemia *may* be a cause of automatism (as we have seen in *Quick* [1973] p 173) the Court of Appeal held that because the evidence showed that for periods of the journey D was in some control, D had been driving without due care and attention, and was not an automaton.

....

What is the difference between insanity and automatism (or between insane automatism and non-insane automatism)?

We have already answered this question when we examined the cases of *Quick* [1973] and *Hennessey* [1989] on p 173. To illustrate it further:

....

R v T [1990] Crim LR 256

D suffered from post-traumatic stress disorder as a consequence of being raped. D stabbed V during a robbery. The application of the external/internal factor test might have resulted in a finding of insanity (the stress disorder), but instead the judge held that the stress was caused by the external factor of the rape and, therefore, the defence was one of automatism.

....

Insanity leads to a verdict of not guilty by reason of insanity. What is the effect of a successful plea of automatism?

We have to give a qualified answer here. The answer is 'it depends on the charge'. The criminal law has separated crimes into those of **specific intent** and those of **basic intent**. If D successfully pleads automatism to a crime of specific intent, he will be acquitted. If D pleads automatism to a crime of basic intent, he is *likely* to be acquitted *unless* he was reckless in becoming an automaton.

What do the terms specific intent and basic intent mean?

There is no single, agreed definition. What we do know is this:

- The correct application of the terms is crucial in applying the defences of automatism and intoxication.

- The terms mean that for some crimes, voluntary intoxication may (rarely) be a defence and automatism is usually a defence.

- The terms relate to the type of *mens rea* in the definition of the offence.

At the most basic level (and if you have done A level Law, you will probably have been taught to this level only), crimes which have a *mens rea* of intention and nothing less are crimes of specific intent, and all other crimes (where recklessness or negligence suffice, and all strict liability crimes) are basic intent. Many students simply learn a list: murder, causing GBH with intent, theft, robbery, and all attempts are crimes of specific intent, and all other crimes are basic intent. *At degree level, this is not enough.*

Revision tip

In *Morgan* [1976] Lord Simon stated specific intent means crimes with an 'ulterior intent'. However, in *Majewski* [1977], the leading case on voluntary intoxication (see 'Key cases', p 183), Lord Simon held that specific intent meant crimes with a 'purposive element'. Then in *Caldwell* [1982], the preferred approach was to look at the wording of the charge. If the charge used the word 'intention' only, it was a specific intent crime; if it used a 'lesser' *mens rea*, or none at all, it was basic.

✔ Looking for extra marks?

First, the definitions given in the cases above are not without critics. All leading textbooks will illustrate their limitations and inconsistencies; and, secondly, the Court of Appeal held in *Heard* [2008] that although the charge was sexual assault which requires intentional touching, the crime is basic intent. This followed the *dicta* of Lord Simon in *Morgan* [1976] because there is no ulterior intent in sexual assault, but it conflicts with the *dicta* in *Caldwell* [1982]. David Ormerod's commentary to the case in the *Criminal Law Review* makes some excellent analytical points which you will do well to understand (see [2007] Crim LR 654).

If D is charged with a specific intent crime and he was an automaton, is he guilty?

No, he is not guilty.

If D is charged with a basic intent crime and he was an automaton, is he guilty?

Usually not; it depends on whether the prosecution can prove D was reckless in becoming an automaton. If he was not reckless, D is to be acquitted.

Bailey [1983] 1 WLR 760

The jury convicted D of assault despite D's evidence that he was hypoglycaemic at the time. D had taken insulin and had failed to eat. The Court of Appeal held that if D realises there is a risk that his conduct (on the facts, failure to eat after taking insulin) may lead to aggressive, unpredictable, and uncontrollable conduct, and he nevertheless deliberately runs the risk, this will amount to recklessness. If D is reckless in becoming an automaton, he cannot succeed with the defence if charged with a basic intent crime.

Revision tip

Pay attention to the precise wording of the test. It is not simply 'Was D reckless when he became an automaton (say, when he took the insulin)?' but 'Did he realise before becoming an automaton that his conduct may lead him to be aggressive, unpredictable, and uncontrollable?'

Does the defence of automatism negate the definitional elements of the offence?

There is no authoritative answer to that question, but it might not matter. Most legal commentators agree that, at a minimum, the defence negates *actus reus* because the conduct (act or omission) is involuntary in the sense that D has no control over his body. If that is correct, it means the defence is available to crimes of *mens rea* and strict liability (it would not be available to crimes of strict liability if the defence negated *mens rea* only). If the defence does negate *actus reus*, it does not really matter if it negates *mens rea* too.

Intoxication

A note on terminology first: When we use the word **intoxication,** we are restricting our discussion to alcohol and other dangerous drugs such as LSD ('acid'). In the criminal law, the cases use the term 'dangerous drugs' as meaning those commonly known to create states of unpredictability or aggression (*Hardie* [1985]). We will consider what defence applies when D takes a non-dangerous drug later.

Involuntary intoxication

D is **involuntarily intoxicated** when he is not aware he is taking an intoxicant at all, and the best example is where his non-alcoholic drink is laced with alcohol. The law is very straightforward now; even if D was involuntarily intoxicated, if he formed the *mens rea* of the crime, he is guilty. Any lack of moral fault on his part is irrelevant.

> *Revision Lip*
>
> The leading case on involuntary intoxication is ***Kingston*** [1995] which you will find in 'Key cases', p 183. It is a House of Lords case, but the Court of Appeal (reversed by the House of Lords) had taken pity on D, who (it was alleged) was not at fault in becoming intoxicated. You might want to read the judgment of the Court of Appeal and reflect on the view that it is unfair to convict a person who did form *mens rea*, but would not have done if his drink had not been laced.

The distinction between specific and basic intent is *not* relevant where D is involuntarily intoxicated. If D knows he is drinking or taking drugs, but the effect of them is more than he realised, he is voluntarily intoxicated (*Allen* [1988]).

Voluntary intoxication

It is probably best to show you the effect of **voluntary intoxication** first, and unravel the law afterwards.

If D was voluntarily intoxicated with alcohol or a dangerous drug and D is charged with a specific intent crime *and* D did not form *mens rea then* D is not guilty of the specific intent crime (but liability may be reduced).

If D was voluntarily intoxicated with alcohol or a dangerous drug and D is charged with a basic intent crime *then* the jury must ask, would D have formed *mens rea* if sober? If no, D is not guilty. If yes, D is guilty and the prosecution does not have to prove that D did in fact form the *mens rea*.

These statements summarise the law as decided in *Majewski* [1977] and clarified by *Richardson and Irwin* [1999].

It should therefore be clear to you that voluntary intoxication is *not* a defence. At most, intoxication is a reason that the prosecution cannot prove D formed *mens rea*, and this applies only where D is charged with a specific intent crime. If D is charged with a basic intent crime and would have formed *mens rea* if he had been sober, the prosecution does not even have to prove D did form it when intoxicated.

If D does not form the mens rea of a specific intent crime

Where D is voluntarily intoxicated and does not form the *mens rea* of a specific intent crime, D cannot be convicted of that crime, but *if there is a basic intent alternative* offence, he will be convicted of the lesser crime. So if D is charged with murder and did not form *mens rea* due to his intoxication, he will be convicted of manslaughter.

Lipman [1970] 1 QB 152

D killed V by cramming eight inches of bed sheet down her throat. D had voluntarily taken the drug LSD, had no knowledge of what he was doing, and no intention to harm V. The Court of Appeal held that D was correctly convicted of manslaughter.

The reduction of the specific intent crime to the basic intent crime would work very well if every specific intent crime had a basic intent alternative, but they do not (for example, if D is charged with theft but did not form *mens rea* due to voluntary intoxication, he must be acquitted; there is no 'reckless' or basic intent form of theft).

If D drinks or takes drugs in order to commit a specific intent crime (so-called Dutch courage), as a matter of policy the defence fails and there is no reduction in liability to a basic intent crime (*AG for Northern Ireland v Gallagher* [1963]).

D commits a basic intent crime

Strictly, according to *Majewski* [1977], if D was voluntarily intoxicated and is charged with a basic intent crime, he is guilty; no questions asked; no evidence of *mens rea* necessary.

Majewski [1977] AC 443

D was involved in a brawl at a public house in which he assaulted the landlord, customers, and police officers. His defence was that the offences had been committed while he was suffering from the effect of alcohol and drugs. The House of Lords held that if D is charged with a specific intent crime and did not form *mens rea*, he is not guilty of that crime (but liability may be reduced). Voluntary intoxication is not a defence to basic crimes.

However, the jury might have also to consider (if raised by D) whether D would have formed the *mens rea* of the basic intent crime if he had been sober;

Richardson and Irwin [1999] 1 Cr App R 392

V, the defendants, and others were all university students and had been drinking alcohol. They were messing around together, but as part of their horseplay, they lifted V over the edge of a balcony. He was dropped, fell about ten or 12 feet and was injured. The Court of Appeal held that the jury should have been directed to decide whether these particular defendants would have foreseen, had they not been drinking, that their actions might cause injury.

✅ *Looking for extra marks?*

The approach in *Richardson and Irwin* [1999] is preferred to the strict *Majewski* [1977] approach, which simply relieved the prosecution from proving the *mens rea* of a basic intent crime because the *Majewski* [1977] rules concerning basic intent crimes and voluntary intoxication might have been seen as being in conflict with **s 8 Criminal Justice Act 1967** (which you will find in 'How is guilt proved?' in chapter 1, p 6). *Richardson and Irwin* [1999] reconciles the conflict because the jury does have to infer from the evidence that D would have been reckless when sober before they can convict him of the basic intent crime.

In its report, *Intoxication and criminal liability* (Law Com No 314, 2009), the Law Commission proposes the abolition of the terms specific and basic intent, but otherwise approves the *Richardson and Irwin* approach.

Is prescription medication 'dangerous'?

The answer is 'no'. The *Bailey* [1983] rules (see p 177) apply. Prescription medication is dealt with in the same way as a non-dangerous drug, which includes insulin, and soporific (sleep-inducing) drugs, even someone else's and even to excess. Case law is inconsistent in terms of the label attached to the defence; some call it involuntary intoxication (probably because the intoxication by the non-dangerous drug was involuntary); others call it automatism (making a parallel with cases such as *Quick* [1973]) but the outcome is clear, and illustrated by *Hardie* [1985]:

Hardie [1985] 1 WLR 64

D lived with a woman at her flat. When their relationship broke down, D became distraught and took a number of her Valium tablets (a well-known sedative or soporific drug). He started a fire in the flat and was charged with reckless criminal damage. The Court of Appeal held that the jury should have been allowed to consider whether the taking of the Valium was itself reckless.

The reason for this decision is because Valium is not dangerous *per se*, but if D knows its likely effect on him is to make him less inhibited, or aggressive, unpredictable, and uncontrollable, then automatism is not a defence to a crime of basic intent.

Intoxicated mistakes

If D makes a mistake when he is voluntarily intoxicated (when it is of course more likely that mistakes are made) we need to establish the nature of the mistake to see if D has a defence. It is a matter of public policy that the availability of defences is limited where D is drunk.

If D's mistake relates to some element of a statutory provision which is phrased in such a way as to include D's mistake, he may be lucky enough to escape liability. Your attention is drawn to the case of *Jaggard v Dickinson* [1981] in chapter 13, p 159. There is no doubt D would not have made the mistake she did had she been sober, but because s 5 Criminal Damage Act 1971 refers expressly to 'belief', and because D had that belief, she had a lawful excuse.

There are cases which provide that other drunken mistaken beliefs will not afford D a defence, to crimes of either specific or basic intent (*O'Grady* [1987], *O'Connor* [1991], and *Hatton* [2006]) but there are two problems with this approach:

1. the decisions conflict with *Majewski* [1977] because that (authoritative) case provides that if D did not form *mens rea* for a specific intent crime (and a mistake can prevent D from forming *mens rea*) he cannot be guilty of it, and

2. the decisions conflict with *Richardson and Irwin* [1999] because that case provides that for crimes of basic intent, the jury should consider if D would have formed *mens rea* when sober.

Deciding between competing causes

Problem questions often involve a defendant who has been suffering dizzy spells and black-outs, but nevertheless drinks alcohol and commits the *actus reus* of a crime, then trips and bangs his head and commits another crime, and perhaps then is given someone else's sleeping tablets and commits yet another crime. Your job is NOT to decide which defence will succeed, but to explain the defences which will probably be raised, how they are defined in law (using authorities in support), and the likelihood of their success. This will almost always involve defining and applying the distinction between specific intent and basic intent crimes.

Mistake

This defence confuses students, but there is a good way to master it:

1. Most mistakes do not affect liability at all.

2. Mistakes of criminal law do not affect liability because ignorance of the criminal law is no defence.

3. However, mistakes of the civil law (see *Smith* [1974] in chapter 13, p 159) and some mistakes of fact do prevent liability provided D makes the 'right' mistake.

By 'right' mistake, we mean that if D makes a mistake in respect of a definitional element of the *actus reus* and that mistake negates *mens rea*, D is not guilty. The leading case on mistake is *Morgan* [1976] to which we referred in chapter 6, and which you will find in 'Key cases', p 184. The House of Lords held that for the offence of rape as it was then defined, the *actus reus* was intercourse without the consent of V and the *mens rea* was intention to commit the act not caring whether V consented or not. As a matter of legal principle, if D made a mistake which meant D thought V was consenting, D was not guilty, *not* because he had a defence, but because the prosecution could not prove the *mens rea*.

Lord Hailsham explained it like this:

> Once one has accepted, what seems to me abundantly clear, that the prohibited act in rape is non-consensual sexual intercourse, and that the guilty state of mind is an intention to commit it, it seems to me to follow as a matter of inexorable logic that there is no room either for a 'defence' of honest belief or mistake, or of a defence of honest and reasonable belief or mistake. Either the prosecution proves that the accused had the requisite intent, or it does not.

This principle has been echoed in *Kimber* [1983] and in *Beckford* [1988] where Lord Griffiths said that because it is an essential element of all crimes of violence that the violence should be unlawful, if D raises self-defence or mistaken belief that D was acting in self-defence (see chapter 15) it must be disproved by the prosecution or D is entitled to be acquitted.

Revision tip

If you come across a mistake problem question, identify the offence first and write out the definitional elements (the *actus reus* and *mens rea*). Now apply the mistake to the question. Did D make a mistake which was relevant to an element of the *actus reus* (for example did he shoot at a tree, but hit a human being) *and* does that mistake negate *mens rea* (ie if D is charged with murder, intention to kill/cause GBH to a human being)? If so, there is no liability.

Because only a mistake which prevents D from forming *mens rea* negates liability, mistake cannot negate liability in respect of a strict liability crime (or in respect of a strict liability element of the *actus reus*). To this extent, *Prince* (1875), considered in chapter 4 on p 46, is still representative of the law (and you are also referred to *Tolson* (1889) in 'Looking for extra marks?' in chapter 4, p 47).

Mistake and the other defences

The relationship between mistake and other defences (eg duress) is considered in chapter 15 with the other defences to avoid duplication.

 Key cases

Case	Facts	Principle
Bailey [1983] 1 WLR 760	D was convicted of assault despite D's evidence that he was hypoglycaemic at the time. D had taken insulin and had failed to eat.	The Court of Appeal held that if D realises there is a risk that his conduct may lead to aggressive, unpredictable, and uncontrollable conduct, and he nevertheless deliberately runs the risk, this will amount to recklessness. If D is reckless in becoming an automaton, he cannot succeed with the defence if charged with a basic intent crime.
Broome v Perkins (1987) 85 Cr App R 321	D was a diabetic who suffered a hypoglycaemic attack whist driving home. He was able to negotiate road junctions and traffic lights and he veered away from other vehicles. D was charged with driving without due care and attention.	The Court of Appeal held that because the evidence showed that for periods of the journey D was in some control, D had been driving without due care and attention, and was not an automaton.
Hennessey [1989] 1 WLR 287	D was an insulin-dependent diabetic who had not taken insulin and had not eaten for several days. He sought to raise a defence of automatism, in that the offences with which he was charged were committed during a state of hyperglycaemia.	That was an internal cause (the diabetes itself) and not an external cause (the insulin). The correct defence was insanity.
Kingston [1995] 2 AC 355	D had paedophiliac tendencies and was charged with indecent assault on a boy aged 15. D's defence was that he had been drugged by another, X, who had arranged to blackmail D by photographing D in a compromising situation with the boy. D stated that, had he not been drugged, he would not have acted as he did, and that he had no recollection of so acting. The jury was directed that a drugged intent was still an intent. He was convicted.	Although the Court of Appeal had allowed D's appeal because of the apparent absence of moral fault, the House of Lords held where the prosecution proved that the *mens rea* was present when the *actus reus* occurred, the defence of involuntary intoxication could not be open to D.
Majewski [1977] AC 443	D was involved in a brawl at a public house in which he assaulted the landlord, customers, and police officers. His defence was that the offences had been committed while he was suffering from the effect of alcohol and drugs.	If D is charged with a specific intent crime and did not form *mens rea*, he is not guilty of that crime (but liability may be reduced). Voluntary intoxication is not a defence to basic crimes (+ the Richardson and Irwin 'gloss'; if D would have formed the *mens rea* when sober).

Key cases

✳✳✳✳✳✳✳✳✳✳

Case	Facts	Principle
M'Naghten's case (1843) **8 ER 718**	D was suffering from morbid delusions and a persecution syndrome. He fired his gun at the Prime Minister's secretary, believing he was actually shooting the Prime Minister, because M'Naghten believed there was a plot against him.	The House of Lords stated: 'the jury should be directed that every man is presumed to be sane … until the contrary be proved to their satisfaction, and that to establish a defence on the ground of insanity it must be clearly proved that at the time of committing the act the party accused was labouring under such a defect of reason, from disease of the mind, as not to know the nature and quality of the act he was doing, or, if he did know it, that he did not know that he was doing what was wrong.'
Morgan **[1976] AC 182**	D invited X, Y, and Z to his house to have intercourse with his wife, V, telling them that she was kinky, and that if she appeared to resist, it was just pretence. They had intercourse with her, although she struggled and protested. All four were charged with rape. The question on appeal was whether their belief that she consented was a defence.	The House of Lords held that a defendant cannot be convicted of rape if he believed, albeit mistakenly, that the woman consented, even though he had no reasonable grounds for that belief (the reasonableness or otherwise of the alleged belief was important evidence as to whether or not it was truly held).
Quick **[1973] QB 910**	D was a nurse who was charged with assaulting a patient. D, a diabetic, gave evidence that he had taken insulin as prescribed on the morning of the assault, had then drunk alcohol and eaten little food and had no recollection of the assault. He called medical evidence to the effect that he was suffering hypoglycaemia.	The Court of Appeal held that 'disease of the mind' within the meaning of the *M'Naghten Rules*, was a malfunctioning of the mind caused by disease. It did not include the application to the body of some external factor, such as insulin.
Sullivan **[1984] AC 156**	D kicked V in the head and body while suffering an attack of psychomotor epilepsy. D gave evidence, which was not challenged, that he had no recollection of the incident.	The House of Lords accepted that it was regrettable that the label of insanity had to be applied to a case of epilepsy, but D had an internal disorder which impaired D's mental faculties of reason, memory, and understanding.

Key debates

Topic	'Insanity and automatism: pleas for information'
Author/Academic	Andrew Ashworth
Viewpoint	In this Editorial of the journal, the need for an analysis of the practical operation of insanity and non-insane automatism is reviewed. Much needed recommendations for reform must be tailored to the results of the Law Commission consultation and Scoping Paper.
Source	[2012] 10 Crim LR 733

Topic	'The structure of criminal defences'
Author/Academic	William Wilson
Viewpoint	To quote the author, this article seeks to answer this question: 'How do we construct criminal defences in such a way as to reconcile the needs of society on the one hand and justice/fairness to the individual on the other?'
Source	[2005] Crim LR 108

Exam questions

Problem question

Gail was recently diagnosed as diabetic and the doctor explained to her the importance of checking her blood sugar levels and maintaining a balanced diet and eating regularly. She was shown how to check her blood sugar and how to inject insulin. She was also advised to avoid alcohol, or drink in moderation, at least until she was confident about how to manage her diabetes.

Despite the doctor's warnings, Gail went out to party on a Friday night, less than a month after the diagnosis, and she drank a very large volume of alcohol. The following morning, Saturday, Gail was very hung-over and she did not feel able to eat all day. She did, however, check her blood sugar levels and she self-administered insulin.

On the Sunday morning, Gail still felt ill, and did not eat all morning. By midday, she felt a little better, so she decided to go to her local shop to buy some food. She self-administered insulin before she left.

In the shop, Gail pulled electrical items which were on display off the shelves, breaking them. When the store manager approached Gail, she attacked him with a toaster which had been on display, causing serious injuries.

Exam questions

✽✽✽✽✽✽✽✽✽✽

Gail was charged with recklessly destroying property belonging to another contrary to s 1(1) Criminal Damage Act 1971, and causing grievous bodily harm with intent under s 18 Offences Against the Person Act 1861.

Gail has no memory of the events on the Sunday at all. Expert evidence has established she was suffering hypoglycaemia at the time.

Focusing on the availability of a defence, discuss Gail's criminal liability, if any.

How would your answer differ, if at all, if on both Saturday and Sunday, Gail had forgotten to inject herself with insulin and was suffering hyperglycaemia at the relevant time?

An outline answer is included at the end of the book.

Essay question

> ... the nature of 'specific intent' is a matter of great importance but a careful scrutiny of the authorities ... fails to reveal any consistent principle by which specific and basic are to be distinguished. (D. Ormerod, *Smith and Hogan Criminal Law*, OUP, 13th edn, 2011, p 317)

Analyse the defences of voluntary intoxication and non-insane automatism in light of this comment.

Online Resource Centre

To see an outline answer to this question log on to www.oxfordtextbooks.co.uk/orc/concentrate/

#15

Defences II

Key facts

- In this chapter we consider the defences of:
  - consent (which we simply revisit);
  - self-defence (which is using reasonable force in the defence of oneself, others, and/or property, and the prevention of crime); and
  - duress (which consists of being compelled to commit a crime to avoid death or serious harm in a situation of immediacy where there is no route of escape. Duress may also include, or exist separately to, the defence of necessity; an apparent contradiction to which we return on p 197).

- In the criminal law, we distinguish excusatory and justificatory defences. Duress is an excusatory defence; consent and self-defence are justificatory defences. If the defence of necessity does exist separately to the defence of duress, it is a justificatory defence.

- The burden of proof in relation to each defence considered in this chapter lies on the prosecution. That means D carries an evidential burden in relation to the defence(s) but the prosecution has the legal burden of disproof.

Chapter overview

The accepted formula for criminal liability is *actus reus* plus *mens rea* minus defence (see **chapter 1**) and we use this formula to show you how the defences covered in this chapter work:

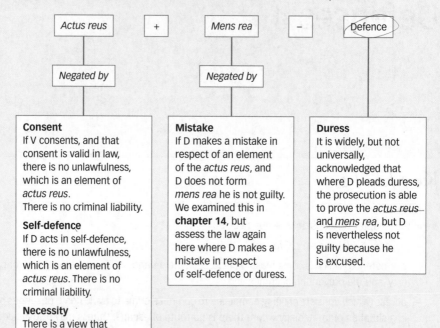

| Actus reus | + | Mens rea | − | Defence |

Negated by (under Actus reus)

Negated by (under Mens rea)

Consent
If V consents, and that consent is valid in law, there is no unlawfulness, which is an element of *actus reus*.
There is no criminal liability.

Self-defence
If D acts in self-defence, there is no unlawfulness, which is an element of *actus reus*. There is no criminal liability.

Necessity
There is a view that necessity has the same effect on criminal liability as consent and self-defence above, that is where D acted in necessity, there is no unlawfulness, which is an element of *actus reus*. There is no criminal liability.

All three 'defences' mentioned here are considered to be **justificatory** defences.

Mistake
If D makes a mistake in respect of an element of the *actus reus*, and D does not form *mens rea* he is not guilty. We examined this in **chapter 14**, but assess the law again here where D makes a mistake in respect of self-defence or duress.

Duress
It is widely, but not universally, acknowledged that where D pleads duress, the prosecution is able to prove the *actus reus* and *mens rea*, but D is nevertheless not guilty because he is excused.

Introduction

We saw in chapter 14 that some defences are said to negate the *actus reus* of the offence, such as automatism. This means D is acquitted because the prosecution cannot prove D satisfies the *actus reus*. Where it is a defence, mistake negates the *mens rea*, so D is not acquitted because he has a self-standing defence, but because the prosecution cannot prove he formed *mens rea*.

There are some defences where D is acquitted because what would otherwise be a crime is justified. For example, an act done in self-defence is justified. Consent is treated in the same way. In fact, it is not quite this simple, and the justificatory defences are often said to negate the *actus reus* (for example, what would be a battery but for self-defence amounts to an application of force, but it is not an application of *unlawful* force, so there is no *actus reus*).

There are, however, some defences which do not negate *actus reus* or *mens rea*, but D is still entitled to be acquitted because his acts are excused, hence the term *excusatory* defences. Duress is an excusatory defence.

Revision tip

You need to know the *elements* of the defences (ie those elements which must be established and the authorities in support), but you also need to know the *effect* of the defence (is D acquitted? is liability reduced?) *and* you need to explain *why* the defence works in the way it does. You should also be very careful when allocating the burden of proof.

Consent

This topic is dealt with in detail in chapters 5 and 6. The consent of the person who would otherwise be the victim without that consent negates the *actus reus* of the unlawfulness of the assault. There is, therefore, no assault. On the whole, V cannot consent to injury but informed consent given by an adult may be valid, subject to the limits on the type and purpose of the activity.

Self-defence and prevention of crime

The law governing the defences of self-defence (why we use the plural 'defences' will be revealed shortly) was consolidated in s 76 Criminal Justice and Immigration Act 2008. Our approach here is to produce each subsection and then illustrate the operation of the defences with decided cases.

Criminal Justice and Immigration Act (CJIA) 2008

Section 76(1) of the Act applies where:

(a) an issue arises as to whether a person charged with the offence ('D') is entitled to rely on a defence within subsection (2), and

(b) the question arises whether the degree of force used by D against a person ('V') was reasonable in the circumstances.

Self-defence and prevention of crime

✶✶✶✶✶✶✶✶✶✶

The defences of self-defence are successful only if the force used by D was 'reasonable'. In most cases, what is reasonable is a simple matter of fact and the jury needs no direction. So if, say, V was physically attacking D, or was about to, then there was clearly a justification if D reacted, and D has a defence if his reaction was reasonable. There is no legal requirement that D must retreat from an attack (*Bird* [1985] and s 76 (6A)) but failure to do so is something the jury can consider when deciding if D used reasonable force. Similarly, D may act pre-emptively (*AG's Ref (No 2 of 1983)* [1984]) but the overriding factor is always whether the action is reasonable. In *Keane* [2010] the Court of Appeal held that an original aggressor *may* even have the defence *if* the original V's response 'was so out of proportion to what the original aggressor did that in effect the roles were reversed'.

Section 76(2) explains why we used the plural (defences) earlier when describing self-defence:

The defences are—

(a) the common law defence of self-defence;

(aa) the common law defence of defence of property; and

(b) the defences provided by section 3(1) of the Criminal Law Act 1967...

The common law defences include using reasonable force to defend oneself, another person, or property from attack or the threat of attack (it is sometimes called private defence). The defence under s 3(1) Criminal Law Act 1967 provides that D may use such force as is reasonable in the circumstances in the prevention of crime or in effecting or assisting in the lawful arrest of offenders.

The defences operate the same rules (*McInnes* [1971]) and in some cases, D will be able to rely on either defence, but there will be times where only one of the defences will be available. For example, if D makes a mistake about the need to use force, his only defence is the common law defence (he cannot act in the prevention of crime under s 3(1) if there is in fact no crime to prevent).

Section 76(3) and (4) start to explain what the legal requirements of reasonable force include:

(3) The question whether the degree of force used by D was reasonable in the circumstances is to be decided by reference to the circumstances as D believed them to be, and subsections (4) to (8) also apply in connection with deciding that question.

(4) If D claims to have held a particular belief as regards the existence of any circumstances—

(a) the reasonableness or otherwise of that belief is relevant to the question whether D genuinely held it; but

(b) if it is determined that D did genuinely hold it, D is entitled to rely on it for the purposes of subsection (3), whether or not—

(i)   it was mistaken, or

(ii) (if it was mistaken) the mistake was a reasonable one to have made.

So if D makes a mistake and believes he is under attack when he is not, he is judged on the facts as he saw them. This is a subjective test and is best illustrated by *Williams (Gladstone)* [1987] which you will find in 'Key cases', p 200, and more recently in *Oye* [2013], in 'Looking for extra marks?', p 192. However, and as we saw in chapter 14, there are sound policy reasons for restricting the availability of defences where D was drunk: see *O'Grady* [1987].

Section 76(5) is as follows:

(5) But subsection (4)(b) does not enable D to rely on any mistaken belief attributable to intoxication that was voluntarily induced.

Section 76(6) also restates the common law, here to the effect that the *amount* of force used is always assessed objectively. In other words, was the amount or degree of force used proportionate, in the light of D's beliefs (including his mistaken beliefs (*Drane* (2008)):

(6) The degree of force used by D is not to be regarded as having been reasonable in the circumstances as D believed them to be if it was disproportionate in those circumstances.

Public and media interest in the issue of how much force may be used against an intruder into one's home produced a new subsection in s 76 under the **Courts and Crime Act 2013**:

(5A) In a householder case, the degree of force used by D is not to be regarded as having been reasonable in the circumstances as D believed them to be if it was grossly disproportionate in those circumstances.

This did not in any way change the law; disproportionate force is not reasonable force. However, it is a little more subtle than that; if D rightly (or wrongly, *Williams*) thinks he is being attacked, but perceives the degree of danger as being greater than would be perceived by a reasonable person, the jury must assess what was *objectively* reasonable. *Martin (Anthony)* [2003] was a very high profile case where D's conviction for murder was substituted with a conviction for manslaughter by way of diminished responsibility (see chapter 7). What is relevant here is why his defence of self-defence failed.

....

Martin (Anthony) [2003] QB 1

D shot two people who were burgling his home. The jury rejected self-defence, presumably because he had used excessive force but, on appeal, expert psychiatric evidence was heard which established D to be suffering from a longstanding paranoid personality disorder. It was D's argument that this disorder had caused him to be mistaken about the amount of force which would be reasonable in the circumstances. The Court of Appeal held that the jury could not, except in exceptional circumstances (which were not explained), take into account D's psychiatric condition for the purpose of deciding whether excessive force had been used.

....

In s 76(7) we see that two considerations are to be taken into account:

(a) that a person acting for a legitimate purpose may not be able to weigh to a nicety the exact measure of any necessary action; and

(b) that evidence of a person's having only done what the person honestly and instinctively thought was necessary for a legitimate purpose constitutes strong evidence that only reasonable action was taken by that person for that purpose.

Self-defence and prevention of crime

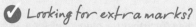

Although the use of reasonable force does *not* involve disproportionate force, D is not expected, in a state of anxiety and in the face of aggression from another, 'to weigh to a nicety the exact measure of any necessary action'. This is a common sense approach and s 76(7) is an exact duplication of the Privy Council decision in *Palmer v R* [1971].

> ✅ *Looking for extra marks?*
>
> In *Oye* [2013], the court had to consider how to deal with a defendant who has an insane delusion which:
>
> **(a)** causes a mistaken belief about an impending attack, and
>
> **(b)** causes a mistaken belief about the degree of force needed to defend oneself from the perceived attack.
>
> The Court of Appeal confirmed the law per *Williams* and **Martin** (above). Can you explain, then, whether the law permits either or both, or neither, mistakes (a) and (b) above to be taken into account for the defence of self-defence? Can you explain why?

For a summary of the defence, see Figure 15.1.

Figure 15.1 'Self'-defence

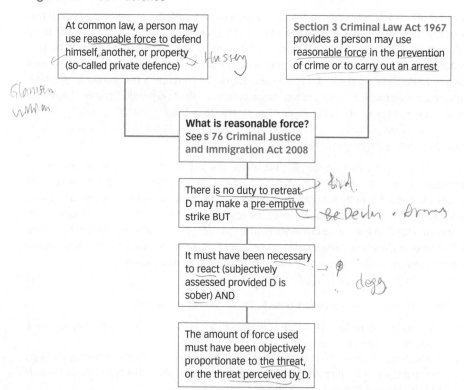

The effect of the defence

We now leave s 76 and the remainder of the defence is examined by case law alone.

If successful, self-defence negates the unlawfulness of the *actus reus* and D must be acquitted. If the defence fails, for example because D used more force than was proportionate (ie excessive force) the defence fails (*Clegg* [1995]). There is no 'half-way house' where excessive force reduces the crime to a lesser offence, such as murder to manslaughter.

Self-defence and the right to life

Where D uses force to defend himself, and kills his attacker in so doing, the attacker's right to life under **Article 2 European Convention on Human Rights** has not been infringed because the attacker's initial act of aggression negated his right. If D used excessive force, of course, D has infringed **Article 2**. What about where D used reasonable force, but was mistaken about the need to use that force? You will recall that he is entitled to be acquitted under the rule in *Williams (Gladstone)* [1987], but he may nonetheless have infringed **Article 2**. This is because under ECHR law, a mistake must be a reasonable one (objectively assessed) rather than just genuinely made (subjectively assessed). There are no cases which deal directly with this point, but see *McCann v UK* (1995) on self-defence and **Article 2** in general, and refer to 'Key debates', p 200.

Duress

There are two types of duress: by threats and of circumstances. The authority for both is *Howe* [1987], approving *Graham* [1982], but the most recent House of Lords case, *Hasan* [2005], has restricted the defence much more than previous decisions, so you must be aware of it.

. . . .

Hasan [2005] 2 AC 467

D pleaded duress to burglary. He claimed a drug dealer with a reputation for violence had threatened that he and his family would be harmed if he did not carry out the burglary. The dealer was the boyfriend of his employer, who ran an escort agency and was involved in prostitution. The House of Lords held that a person cannot rely on the defence of duress if he voluntarily becomes or remains associated with others engaged in criminal activity in a situation where he knows or ought reasonably to know that he may be the subject of compulsion by them or their associates.

. . . .

What is the difference between duress by threats and of circumstances?

If a human coercer says to D 'Burgle that house, or I will beat you up', or 'I will kill you unless you drive my getaway car away from a heist', it is a case of duress by threats. That is not to say the defence will succeed, just to show the type of threat which may put D in a state of duress. On the other hand, D may feel that circumstances compel him to act, but there is no actual threat. For example, D is driving his car through an area of the city which he knows to have a very high violent crime rate. He is stationary at traffic lights, and three men approach his car and beckon him. Thinking he is about to be car-jacked or attacked, D drives through the red lights. This is an example of where D might plead the other type of duress: that of circumstances. The Court of Appeal accepted that there is this variation on 'traditional' duress (by threats) in *Conway* [1989], again in *Martin* (1989), and then in *Pommell* [1995].

The two forms of the defence operate in the same way and are available as defences to the same crimes as each other. Therefore, to keep matters simple, we will refer to 'threats' throughout the rest of this chapter and will not keep repeating 'or circumstances'. Of course, we will specify where an aspect applies only to one of the forms of the defence. But, wherever you see reference to threats, remember that the defence applies equally where D acts as a result of the circumstances. Note also that the authorities cited may be from either form of the defence.

The elements of duress

The defence is very difficult to plead successfully, but broadly speaking there are two elements (*Howe* [1987]):

1. was D, or might he have been, induced to act as he did because, as a result of what he reasonably believed, D had good cause to fear that if he did not so act the threatener would kill him or cause him serious physical injury, or in the circumstances, he might die or suffer serious injury; and, if the answer is yes,

2. would a sober person of reasonable firmness, sharing D's characteristics, have done the same? If yes, the defence may succeed.

However, in addition to the two elements above:

- there must be immediacy;
- D must not have missed an opportunity to escape the threat without committing a crime; and
- if D foresaw or ought reasonably to have foreseen the risk of being subjected to any compulsion by threats of violence (not just crimes of the kind with which the defendant was charged), the defence fails.

The reason for all of these limitations on this defence is one of policy, in that the defence should be very difficult to plead successfully, lest it become 'a charter for terrorists, gang-leaders and kidnappers' according to Lord Simon in *DPP for Northern Ireland v Lynch* [1975].

Revision tip

To maximise marks, you have to adopt a methodical approach when answering problem questions on duress. There are a lot of elements and a lot of reasons why the defence may fail.

The 'subjective' test

An overborne will

Defendants who plead the defence successfully were usually in a state of such acute anxiety that they were compelled to commit a crime because they (reasonably) saw no way out of their predicament, and if they did not act immediately, death or serious harm would have resulted. That is why we say D's will was overborne (Lord Simon in *DPP for Northern Ireland v Lynch* [1975]). If the jury believes D was not actually compelled to act because of the threat, the defence fails at the first hurdle.

Good cause to fear

If D thought that he was being threatened, but he was not, his mistake does not prevent the defence succeeding, provided the mistake was a reasonable one. Suppose D was threatened by C, a man with a reputation for violence, to commit a crime or be killed. Even if C did not intend to kill D if D did not do as C said, D could still plead duress as his mistake is reasonable (provided the defence does not fail for another reason, of course). In some other defences, a mistake as to an element of the defence, especially the 'subjective' element, negates liability whether the mistake was reasonable or not (eg *Williams (Gladstone)* [1987] mentioned on p 200). Not so here (*Hasan* [2005]).

Threat etc of death or serious injury

The defence fails unless there has been a threat of death or serious physical injury (*Baker and Wilkins* [1997], *van Dao* [2012]), but once there has been such a threat, the defence may be available if D's motivation for committing the crime was cumulative and also involved a fear of something else, such as C revealing D's sexual orientation to his family (*Valderrama-Vega* [1985]).

Threat etc to whom?

In *Hasan* [2005], Lord Bingham said that the threat must be directed against D or his immediate family, or someone close to him (*Wright* [2000]) or, if not, to a person for whose safety D would reasonably regard himself as responsible.

··

Conway [1989] QB 290

This was the first time the Court of Appeal expressly approved the defence of duress of circumstances; D was charged with reckless driving. The passenger in D's car, T, had previously been the target of a gun attack. When two men approached D's car, he feared that T was about to be shot at again, and he drove away, recklessly. Neither D nor T realised that the men were plainclothes police officers. Allowing his appeal, the Court of Appeal held that the defence was available where D could be said from an objective standpoint to be acting in order to avoid death or serious injury, to himself, or another for whose safety D would reasonably regard himself as responsible. As his passenger, T was such a person.

··

Duress

✳✳✳✳✳✳✳✳✳✳

The person of reasonable firmness

The jury must be satisfied that a hypothetical person with a reasonably firm temperament would have done what D did. The question which always arises with the reasonable person is what, if any, of D's characteristics are relevant in determining this element?

The answer is: none that affect the essence of the reasonable firmness of the defendant. Therefore, characteristics which can *not* be given to the reasonable person include vulnerability or pliancy (*Horne* [1994]), emotional instability (*Hegarty* [1994]), drug addiction (*Flatt* [1996]), or even low IQ (*Bowen* [1996]). On the other hand, characteristics that are recognised to affect the reasonable firmness of all people, or groups of people, may be relevant, such as age, sex, physical health, pregnancy, and 'learned helplessness' from battered wife syndrome (*Emery* (1993)).

Immediacy

Previous Court of Appeal cases held that the threat against D or another had to be 'imminent', which was interpreted to mean 'such that it operated on his mind so as to overbear his will' (*Abdul-Hussain* [1999]). However, in *Hasan* [2005], Lord Bingham, when discussing whether or not D should have escaped the threat by, for example, going to the police, spoke of D reasonably expecting the death or harm to follow *immediately or almost immediately* on his failure to comply with the threat. He also spoke of threats which could be carried out 'there and then'.

Escape

The House of Lords in *Hasan* [2005] overruled the Court of Appeal's decision in *Hudson and Taylor* [1971].

....

Hudson and Taylor [1971] 2 QB 202

Two defendants had committed perjury. They pleaded duress on the basis that they were scared of physical recrimination if they had told the truth. The Court of Appeal allowed their appeals against conviction because, even though the coercer was in the public gallery of the court room where there were police officers, the threat could have been carried out later that day outside court. It was, therefore, not reasonable for the defendants to have escaped the threat.

Lord Bingham in *Hasan* said the decision in *Hudson* had 'the unfortunate effect of weakening the requirement that execution of a threat must be reasonably believed to be ... immediate if it is to support a plea of duress'.

....

Voluntary association in criminal activity

If a person voluntarily becomes or remains associated with others engaged in criminal activity in a situation where he knows or ought reasonably to know that he may be the subject of compulsion to commit crime by them or their associates, he cannot rely on the defence of duress. He need not know that he may be subjected to threats to commit a crime of a particular type, such as the one with which he is now charged (*Hasan* [2005]).

Nominated crime

This applies to duress by threats only. In *Cole* [1994], the Court of Appeal held that D must commit 'the very offence' nominated by the person making the threats. If, for example, D pleads duress to a theft charge where C told him to 'Get me a new TV and DVD player or I'll cut your child up with a knife', as ghastly as that sounds, the defence of duress must fail because C did not order a crime to be committed. D could have bought the TV and DVD player; there was no need to break the law. On the other hand, the defence will not necessarily fail if C tells D to steal a TV and DVD etc even if the make, model, or store from which the theft must occur is not exactly specified (*Ali* (1994)).

Availability of the defence

Duress is a defence to all crimes except murder (whether as principal or as an accessory, *Howe* [1987]), attempted murder, and treason. It *may* be a defence to conspiracy to commit murder (*Ness* [2011]).

Reform

In its report *Murder, manslaughter and infanticide* (Law Com No 304, 2006), the Law Commission recommended making duress generally available to all homicides, as well as all other crimes. In *Hasan* [2005], Lord Bingham noted that 'the logic of this argument is irresistible'. The person of reasonable firmness would be replaced with a person of ordinary courage, and the Law Commission recommended a change to the allocation of the burden of proof (where D merely has to raise duress as a live issue and it is for the prosecution to disprove it) and place the legal burden of proving the defence on the defendant. It is generally considered that this would breach **Article 6(2) ECHR** (the presumption of innocence), and Lord Bingham was very critical of this part of the proposal in *Hasan* [2005].

Necessity

Revision tip

Many students shy away from this topic because of its uncertain existence, but you should persevere. If the exam question is an essay, and you can explain the uncertainties and complexities, presenting the arguments clearly, high marks await you. Remember it is not your job to define the law, but to present to the reader what the current state of the law is, or may be, and what the critical comments on that are.

The first problem is whether necessity exists separately to duress. In many of the cases cited on p 193 onwards for duress, the appellate courts used the terms necessity and duress synonymously. For example, in *Conway* [1989], the Court of Appeal held that the trial judge should have allowed D to plead *necessity* as the defence is available where *duress of circumstances* was established. (See also the Court of Appeal's decision in *Shayler* [2001], which did the same and even though the House of Lords refused to endorse the Court of Appeal on this issue, it did nothing to clarify the position.) However, as we shall see, most academic authors writing on this topic persuasively argue that the two defences (necessity and duress) are not the same.

The second problem is that, if it does exist, it is unclear what the definition of and boundaries to the defence actually are, or should be. This is because of the criminal law's reluctance to accept the existence of this defence outside medical situations. For example, in *Re F (Mental Patient: Sterilisation)* [1990], Lord Goff applied the doctrine of necessity to provide a legal justification for the sterilisation of a mentally incapable adult without her consent. However, one of the most famous criminal law cases ever, that of *Dudley and Stephens* (1884–85), seems to doubt the existence of the defence at all, or at least its application to murder.

....

Dudley and Stephens (1884–85) LR 14 QBD 273

The defendants were sailors, and were cast away in a storm on the high seas. After 20 days at sea, and seven days without food and five without water, the defendants killed the cabin boy who had been shipwrecked with them and fed on his flesh for four days. The jury found that at the time of the killing there was no sail in sight nor any reasonable prospect of relief and that under these circumstances there appeared to the defendants every probability that unless they then or very soon fed upon the boy, or one of themselves, they would die of starvation. However, Lord Coleridge held that upon these facts, there was no proof of any such necessity as could justify the prisoners in killing the boy, and that they were guilty of murder.

....

On the one hand, this case seems to hold that the defence failed, not that it did not exist. On the other hand, Lord Coleridge also said that '... the broad proposition that a man may save his life by killing, if necessary, an innocent and unoffending neighbour ... certainly is not law at the present day', appearing to rule that necessity is never a defence to murder. Then in *London Borough of Southwark v Williams* [1971] Lord Denning explicitly held that:

> Our English law does not admit the defence of necessity ... The reason is because, if hunger were once allowed to be an excuse for stealing, it would open a way through which all kinds of disorder and lawlessness would pass ... Necessity would open a door which no man could shut.

More recently, however, Brooke LJ in *Re A (Children) (Conjoined Twins: Surgical Separation)* [2001] reviewed all previous authorities, and stated that the rule as found in *Dudley and Stephens* was not conclusive on the matter, and implicitly therefore, neither was Lord Denning in *Williams*. *Re A* can be found in 'Key cases', p 199.

Brooke LJ's decision in *Re A* is only persuasive precedent in criminal proceedings, but it does appear to accept that the defence of necessity exists outside the limits of the defence of duress. The *obiter dicta* with respect to the criminal law (Ward and Walker LJJ agreeing with Brooke LJ in this regard) was that the operation would not constitute murder since the three components of the doctrine of necessity were satisfied, namely that:

1. the act was required to avoid inevitable and irreparable evil;

2. no more would be done than was reasonably necessary for the purpose to be achieved; and

3. the evil to be inflicted was not disproportionate to the evil avoided.

✔️ *Looking for extra marks?*

Necessity may be a defence available, subject to the facts, to all crimes. David Ormerod has argued very persuasively that the defence ought to exist. See 'Key debates', p 200. It may, however, not be a defence to criminal liability at all. At the time of updating to the 4th edition of this book (1st January 2014), arguments had been presented to the UK Supreme Court, but judgment had not been given, in the case of *Nicklinson v Ministry of Justice*, a case about necessity and assisted suicide. If you are asked an essay question discussing this defence, you should be prepared to offer the examiner an insight into the decision (presuming it will be delivered by then).

✳️ *Key cases*

Case	Facts	Principle
Hasan [2005] 2 AC 467	D pleaded duress to burglary. He claimed a drug dealer with a reputation for violence had threatened that he and his family would be harmed if he did not carry out the burglary. The dealer was the boyfriend of his employer, who ran an escort agency and was involved in prostitution.	If a person voluntarily becomes or remains associated with others engaged in criminal activity in a situation where he knows or ought reasonably to know that he may be the subject of compulsion by them or their associates, he cannot rely on the defence of duress. Note that the case also contains important *obiter* statements in relation to many of the other elements to the defence.
Re A (Children) (Conjoined Twins: Surgical Separation) [2001] 2 WLR 480	The parents of six-week-old Siamese twins, Mary and Jodie, appealed against a ruling granting medical staff authority to proceed with surgical separation. Mary had severe brain abnormalities, no lung tissue, and no properly functioning heart. The blood supply keeping Mary alive emanated from Jodie who was in all other essential respects functioning and developing normally.	The doctors' acts of separation would not amount to murder because the act was required to avoid inevitable and irreparable evil; no more would be done than was reasonably necessary for the purpose to be achieved, and the evil to be inflicted was not disproportionate to the evil avoided.

Key debates

****

Case	Facts	Principle
Williams (Gladstone) [1987] 3 All ER 411	D saw a third party, V, arresting a youth, X. V said he was a police officer but failed to produce a warrant card. D wrongly thought that X was being unlawfully assaulted by V, and D assaulted V.	The Court of Appeal quashed D's conviction. Where a defendant made a mistake about the need to use force (to defend himself or another), he was to be judged according to his mistaken view of the facts, whether or not that mistake was reasonable. This is a subjective test.

Key debates

Topic	Self-defence and its relationship to the European Convention
Author/Academic	Andrew Ashworth
Viewpoint	A careful analysis of the effects of the **Human Rights Act 1998** on the substantive criminal law, including a useful summary of self-defence and the argument that English law conflicts with **Article 2 ECHR**.
Source	'The Human Rights Act and the substantive criminal law: a non-minimalist view' [2000] Crim LR 564.

Topic	The defences of duress of circumstance and necessity; the same or different?
Author/Academic	David Ormerod
Viewpoint	The defence of necessity does exist or at least should.
Source	'Necessity of circumstance', commentary to *Quayle* at [2006] Crim LR 148; see also *Gardner* [2005] Crim LR 371.

(?) Exam questions

Problem question

Harley received a telephone call at work from his son's school teacher informing him that his son, Ike, had been injured at school and had been taken to the Accident and Emergency Department at the local hospital. The teacher had been told to telephone Harley urgently to secure his attendance at the hospital in case his consent was needed for any medical procedure on Ike. Harley left work immediately and drove, as quickly as possible, to the hospital.

On arrival outside the hospital, Harley was stopped by a security guard, Jed, standing by the side of a barrier, who asked him where he was going in order to advise him on the best car park to use. Harley said very quickly that it was an emergency, and that he did not care which car park he had to use, but he had to get to the Accident and Emergency Department urgently. Jed told Harley to calm down, and that he would be able to find a car park space if Harley could just wait a couple of minutes.

Harley put his car into gear and drove at the barrier, smashing it. He parked his car outside the Accident and Emergency Department in the ambulance bay, and ran into the hospital. As soon as he entered the Department, another security guard, Kody, shouted that Harley had to stop and could not park his car there. Harley punched Kody several times causing serious injuries.

Harley found his son, and discovered there was no real emergency. Ike had, in fact, merely bruised his shin in a football game.

Harley has been charged with intentionally destroying property belonging to another, contrary to s 1(1) **Criminal Damage Act 1971**, in respect of the hospital barrier, and causing grievous bodily harm with intent, contrary to s **18 Offences Against the Person Act 1861**, in respect of the injuries to Kody. Harley intends to plead duress.

Comment on the likely success of the defence.

Would it change your answer if Kody had died and Harley had been charged with murder?

An outline answer is included at the end of the book.

Essay question

The judges seem unable to decide whether the defence of necessity does exist as a form of duress, or does not exist at all.

Consider the truth of this statement.

Online Resource Centre

To see an outline answer to this question log on to www.oxfordtextbooks.co.uk/orc/concentrate/

Exam essentials

Common pitfalls to avoid

Make sure you learn a legal principle for every case you revise. Far too often, assessors face pages and pages of case facts, told as stories, rather than explanations of the law from the cases. This is particularly so in the consent questions, but is not limited to consent.

For crimes with both *actus reus* and *mens rea*, please make sure you know and are able to recite all relevant elements: it is particularly common in the non-fatal offences against the person that the *mens rea* elements are omitted although the *actus reus* elements are well understood, illustrated with case law, and applied to the question, so it is not a weakness in legal knowledge by the student, but exam skills. Where a question involves complex causation issues, do not focus just on causation. Causation is one element of all result crimes; the word 'crimes' being the most important here. What offence has potentially been committed? Have you remembered to state the offence in question, not just one element of it? For example, establishing D caused V's death does not establish which homicide offence has been committed. Having said that, when the question clearly focuses on causation, you should devote an appropriate amount of time to address this.

Boosting marks

When you revise cases, learn the case name, the brief facts, and then ask yourself what is the relevance of the case in law. Ask yourself why you are revising that case; what legal authority or principle does it provide? This will keep you focused and avoid you reciting the case facts without mention of the law. It is also important, particularly for essay questions, to have some awareness of the order in which the cases were decided and of their authority (*stare decisis*). You could use postcards with headings: name; facts; legal principle. But revising knowledge is only part of good exam preparation. The best way to maximise your marks is to plan *practice* into your revision period. Once you have mastered the cases and legislation, put yourself into exam conditions (this takes a huge amount of willpower) and write full answers to a past paper. Try to replicate the requirements of your exam if possible (so, say, do four questions from the paper, or three; whatever is required in your exam). Try your hardest to use questions with which you are *un*familiar. After you have finished (very well done), leave your script alone for a couple of days, then mark it yourself. Use your revision notes and a textbook to check your answer makes sense, includes the key cases, deals with the main points of fact and law. Reflect on what you did well, and what you need to improve. You can learn so much about your own exam style from this simple (but not easy) exercise. Were you strict enough with yourself on how you managed your time? (This is the single biggest problem students have in exams; you have to be in control of the time, and not the other way around.) If you do spot a weakness in technique, or in your criminal law knowledge, you should refer to the advice and online tests in the online resources which accompany this book, which you will find at www.oxfordtextbooks.co.uk/orc/concentrate/. You might (instead or as well) choose to team up with another student on your course and agree to attempt a question and then mark each other's answers.

In the exam make sure you read the question very carefully indeed. It is easy to miss the significance of a seemingly irrelevant or innocuous fact when writing up your answer. I often advise students to sit on their hands when reading the exam questions. Do not start to make notes or jot down plans until you are sure you have understood and thought about what the question is asking. Also make sure you read the rubric (the instructions) because if you are asked to advise the Crown Prosecution Service, then please do. The rubric might ask you to consider the defences only, or murder only, or theft only, or theft and fraud. You risk missing marks if you don't do what you have been asked; and you risk wasting time including irrelevant material in your answer which will not gain you any marks.

Linked topics

All of the defences in the criminal law are defences to liability, and liability is based on an offence. So, if you are revising the defences (any of them), you need a basically good knowledge of the offences that you are likely to be asked about. Voluntary intoxication works well with both the homicides (murder and manslaughter) and the non-fatal offences (ss 18 and 20 or 47 Offences Against the Person Act 1861) because of the distinction between specific and basic intent crimes. Self-defence works well with the non-fatal offences too, especially when you are weighing the proportionality of a reaction against an offence of GBH or ABH or either of the common law crimes. Bear in mind that some defences are not available to certain crimes (eg duress and murder) and some defences are only available to a charge of murder (ie loss of control and diminished responsibility), so factor this into your revision too.

Outline answers

The aim of the following sample answers is to show you how to break down the questions in order to answer them successfully. They in no way presume to be model answers.

Chapter 2

Problem answer

The answer to this question can be broken down into two main parts, but they are not of equal sizes, and the first (*actus reus*) can further be split into three. The second (*mens rea*) is dealt with below, in the answer to the question in chapter 3.

For our purposes (the crime of murder is described in full in chapter 7), there is a single issue for our consideration; did Andrew cause Kirin's death?

Using the flowchart on p 21, Figure 2.1, there are three stages to your answer:

1. *But for* A's act would K have died?

• Explain the *but for* test, and apply it. *But for* A throwing the book, striking K, she would not have died when she did. He is the factual cause of her death.

2. Did A cause K's death in law?

• Remember that all you have to do is find A made a substantial contribution to K's death, and his act need not be the only or even the main cause of her death, provided it is more than 'trifling'. A has made a substantial contribution to her death because his act was a more than slight or trifling cause of her death.

3. Is there a *novus actus interveniens* which breaks the chain of causation (and therefore relieves A of liability)?

• First, consider if the acts of Sandeep and Samantha (making parallels with the case of *Smith* (1959)) break the chain.

• Secondly, consider if the doctor's negligence in misreading the scan was so potent etc: *Cheshire* [1991], *Jordan* (1956). In light of the fact that this was a wholly unnecessary operation, you might feel the causal chain is broken, but on the other hand, D was liable for

murder in *Cheshire* [1991] despite the original injuries being healed.

• Finally, consider whether turning off the machines breaks the causal chain, which it does not (*Malcherek* [1981]).

• So, the *actus reus* of murder might be satisfied, subject to your conclusion on the negligence of the doctor. We cannot yet conclude as to Andrew's liability, however, because we have not yet examined *mens rea*.

Chapter 3

Problem answer

The charge is murder, for which the *mens rea* is intention to kill or cause serious harm (see chapter 7). We are told expressly that Andrew had intent to cause serious harm, *so there is no need to consider indirect intent at all*.

However, because Andrew's intent was against Mark, and he accidentally hit Kirin, you have to explain the doctrine and use the case of *Latimer* (1886) to transfer the malice.

Chapter 4

Problem answer

In order to answer this question, you must appreciate that the word 'knowingly' in s 141 Licensing Act 2003 attaches to the *sale* of the alcohol (and on the facts Alex has conceded that he knew he had sold Bert several alcoholic drinks). The issue is therefore whether Alex can be convicted even though he did not consider whether Bert was drunk (ie whether *that* element is strict liability), or if the prosecution would have to prove Alex knew or realised Bert was drunk (ie that element has a *mens rea* requirement).

Next you must explain that the starting point for making this decision is that there is a presumption of *mens rea* even where that part of the provision in question is silent as to *mens rea* (*Sweet v Parsley* [1970]). That presumption may be displaced (using the reasoning in *Gammon* [1985]) where the offence is

Outline answers
✳✳✳✳✳✳✳✳✳✳

regulatory (not a 'true' crime) and if it is a necessary implication on the wording of the provision (*B v DPP* [2000]). Although to reach a conclusion on the seriousness of the crime, we would need further information regarding the sentence (*Muhamad* [2003]), we could draw a parallel between this offence and selling unsound meat (*Callow v Tillstone* (1900)) and selling lottery tickets to children (*Shah* [2000]), where the offences were strict liability. Further, this crime clearly involves public safety, so if, in the court's view, making the crime one of strict liability would ensure greater vigilance and act as a deterrent to others, the element relating to the drunkenness of the purchaser of the alcohol is more likely to be strict liability (*Blake* [1997]). On this reasoning, Alex will be convicted and the prosecution does not have to prove Alex knew, thought, or even suspected Bert was drunk when Alex sold him the alcohol. Any evidence of no fault on Alex's part is inadmissible (*Sandhu* [1997]).

Chapter 5

Problem answer

Jon

First consider whether Jon's silent telephone calls and knocking at the front door amount to technical assaults (*Ireland* [1998]). Celia must apprehend violence immediately (and this is worth exploring on the facts) and Jon must intend (not on these facts) or foresee her fear of immediate application of harm (which is unlikely). It is also worth pointing out that anxiety related neurosis is unlikely to amount to ABH under s 47 Offences Against the Person Act 1861.

If your syllabus includes the Protection from Harassment Act 1997, you will also be expected to consider whether his conduct is a 'course' which he knows (almost certainly not) or ought to know (note this is objective and might be satisfied) will amount to harassment or cause fear (ss 2 and 4).

Michael

In calling her name, did he commit a technical assault or even s 47 against Celia? It is unlikely, and even if he causes harm and C certainly apprehends it (and immediately), he lacks *mens rea*.

Chapter 6

Problem answer

Please note first that the instructions direct you to consider offences under the Sexual Offences Act 2003 (SOA 2003), so you should not spend time considering the non-fatal and non-sexual offences (such as battery).

Barbara

Andrew could be liable for sexual assault contrary to s 3 SOA 2003. The prosecution would have to prove that Andrew intentionally touched Barbara (which is clearly stated in the facts), the touching was sexual, Barbara did not consent, and Andrew did not reasonably believe she consented. Section 78 SOA 2003 provides that touching is sexual if a reasonable person would consider it to be sexual because of its nature (stroking hair is not sexual per se), or because of its nature, circumstances, or the purpose of any person in relation to it, it is sexual. Andrew's comments regarding Barbara's prettiness can be taken into account by the jury when determining if the touching was sexual or not. As to Barbara's consent, the conclusive presumptions in s 76 SOA 2003 do not apply because there are no deceptions, and there are no evidential presumptions under s 75 on these facts. Section 74 provides that a person consents if he agrees by choice, and has the freedom and capacity to make that choice. Even though Barbara might have felt uncomfortable, and always provided Barbara had capacity to consent, the prosecution might have difficulty proving she did not consent because she did not tell Andrew to stop. Similarly, there may be problems proving Andrew's lack of reasonable belief in Barbara's consent. Although the jury is able to take into account all the circumstances, including any steps Andrew took to ascertain if Barbara was consenting (and he did not ask permission), Andrew might have thought Barbara would not mind, and when she did not object, his belief was confirmed.

Cindy

The complaint is of rape contrary to s 1 SOA 2003. Andrew is male and he intentionally penetrated Cindy's vagina with his penis. The contentious issues again are consent and whether Andrew reasonably believed in that consent. The conclusive presumptions in s 76 do not apply because there are no deceptions, and although Cindy was 'dizzy, sick and disorientated', she was not asleep nor unconscious, so the evidentiary presumptions in s 75 do not apply. We must therefore consider s 74 and also the recent decision of *Bree* [2008]. Even if Cindy was influenced by the drug, she was able to consent if she retained the freedom and capacity to make a choice. Her agreement was reluctant, but she did agree. The jury may feel, however, that even if she did consent, Andrew's belief in her consent was not reasonable. Section 1(2) SOA 2003 provides that whether a belief is reasonable is to be determined having regard to all the circumstances, and Cindy has told Andrew she feels 'very funny' and, as a medical professional, Andrew must know the effect an anaesthetic may have on a patient.

Chapter 7

Problem answer

This question focuses on *mens rea*, and the crime is specified so you must not consider offences other than murder. In order to find liability, you do have to state the *actus reus* and apply it very quickly, but do not linger on distractions (such as causation). Move on to the *mens rea* as soon as possible. There is no evidence of direct intent (due to the phone call), so what about indirect intent? Use the full direction from *Woollin* [1999], and add to it if you have time, by referring to *Re A* [2001] and *Matthews* [2003], but if you have read *Woollin* [1999], you will know that Lord Steyn discussed the liability of the terrorist who telephones a warning, and he concluded that is an example of recklessness, but not intention. You will be expected to give reasons in full.

Chapter 8

Problem answer

You have been instructed to consider gross negligence manslaughter only, so do not get distracted by any other form of unlawful homicide. You should tackle this question only if you are sure you have a clear understanding of the *Adomako* [1994] test, and remember that

it is not sufficient for the offence of gross negligence manslaughter for you to suggest the offence consists merely of the breach of a duty of care, causing death. This is no more than negligence in the law of torts. Without some comment on the essence of the seriousness, the grossness, or the criminality of the act or omission, an answer will struggle to pass.

With regard to the defendant Robert in scenario 1, he is a teacher *in loco parentis* and therefore owes a duty. However, it was not his failure to bring armbands which is the negligence causing death, but allowing Alicia to swim. Anyone can forget to take armbands; but the question is whether she should have been allowed to swim, and if the breach of duty involved an obvious risk of death and was grossly negligent.

The situation in scenario 2 is similar to breach of contract gross negligence cases such as *Pittwood* (1902) and on the facts, the obvious risk of death (*Misra* [2005]) might be more easily established. That said, and it is a question of fact, but this may amount to civil negligence rather than criminal.

In scenario 3, there is no duty to assist because there is no creation of danger by D (*Miller* [1983]) and no other close relationship. In the alternative scenario, however, once he helps, he assumes the duty (*Stone* [1977]) and he breaches it if there is an obvious risk of death and his conduct is so gross to be manslaughter. The jury may feel that such a rescuer should not be punished for trying to help.

Chapter 9

Problem answer

This is a problem question that tests you across the range of inchoate offences and also requires you to judge whether liability can be incurred where the principal (aimed) offence is impossible (because the victim died).

1. Paul for intentionally encouraging the offence of causing grievous bodily harm with intent, contrary to s 44 of the Serious Crime Act 2007. This offence is one of three which has replaced the common law offence of incitement, and liability is not dependent on the full offence being committed or factually possible. The *actus reus* consists of doing an

act which is capable of encouraging an offence and the *mens rea* is where D intends to encourage its commission. In directing Ron to 'beat up' Mark, this offence is satisfied.

2. Paul and Ron for conspiracy to commit GBH with intent. This would be a statutory conspiracy contrary to s 1 of the Criminal Law Act 1977 because Paul and Ron agreed (Ron reluctantly, but agreed nonetheless) to a course of conduct to be pursued which, if the agreement had been carried out in accordance with their intentions, would have (but for its factual impossibility) (*Siracusa* (1990)) amounted to the commission of an offence contrary to s 18 of the Offences Against the Person Act 1861 (see chapter 5) by Ron.

3. Ron and Sam for attempting to commit grievous bodily harm with intent. Attempts are governed by the Criminal Attempts Act 1981. According to Lord Bridge in *Shivpuri* [1987], the offence consists of an act which is more than merely preparatory to the commission of an offence done with the intention of committing an offence, notwithstanding that the commission of the actual offence was, on the facts, impossible. In relation to Ron and Sam, the jury should consider two questions:

- Did they intend to commit the offence which it is alleged they attempted to commit? It is clear they intended to beat Mark up once they got into his house.
- Did they, in relation to that offence, do an act which was more than merely preparatory to the commission of the *intended* offence? It is clear that they broke in, but had not started on any crime of violence when Mark had a heart attack and died. Whether or not an act is merely preparatory, or more than that, is a question of fact for the jury and you should refer to the decisions in *Jones* [1990], *Gullefer* [1990], *Campbell* [1991], and *Geddes* [1996] to reach an informed conclusion.

Chapter 10

Problem answer

Steve has been convicted of murder as principal offender. Murder is therefore the principal offence.

Kieran

K entered a joint venture with S to cause grievous bodily harm to D. Although K did not intend D's death, he almost certainly foresaw that S would intentionally cause D GBH, and assuming K knew of the iron bar, K would probably also have known that the weapon would be used in the crime. S's acts are therefore unlikely to be regarded as fundamentally different from acts in K's contemplation (*Powell, English* [1999]). It is now irrelevant if S acted with more *mens rea* than K foresaw, provided K foresaw the act committed by S (*Rahman* [2008], *Willett* [2011]).

Running from the house would not be sufficient withdrawal in these circumstances (*Becerra* (1975)).

Cooper

C agreed to aid a burglary committed without weapons. There is therefore no common intention in respect of the murder. Liability needs to be considered under the rules governing accessories. Section 8 of the Accessories and Abettors Act 1861 provides that an accessory is liable to be charged and tried as principal. To confirm, murder is the principal offence, so C has aided murder by acting as a lookout. The *actus reus* is not in doubt (we suggest aiding or abetting) but the *mens rea* is less straightforward on these facts. C might have foreseen the type of crime that might be committed (*Bainbridge* [1960], *Bryce* [2004]), and, as C was aware of S's and K's reputation for violence, C would be liable if murder was within a range of crimes C contemplated might be committed. This is especially so, given S's ambiguous comment 'just in case' (*Maxwell* [1978]).

Even if C satisfies the *actus reus* and *mens rea* requirements for being an accessory to murder, he might have made an effective withdrawal in telephoning the police before the completion of the crime. Although *Becerra* (1975) specifies the withdrawal must be communicated to the other parties, as a matter of principle, it must surely be effective where the matter is communicated to the police in order that an arrest can be made.

Chapter 11

Problem answer

First define theft under s 1 Theft Act 1968. Next think about which of the elements the examiner is looking for you to consider in each part—it is unlikely all five elements will have to be discussed in detail in each part, so select your material wisely.

The first part is asking for a careful consideration of the leading cases on appropriation (*Lawrence* [1972], *Morris* [1984], and *Gomez* [1993]). It is also sensible to point out that it is property, which belongs to another, B has an intention not to pay but shows, by paying for the goods (*Ghosh* [1982]), that he realises ordinary honest people would regard him as dishonest. In theory, it does not matter that he goes on to pay for them, although he would be unlikely to be prosecuted as there is no overt act of theft.

The second part concerns coincidence in time of the *actus reus* and *mens rea*. C is not liable when she leaves the store because she is not dishonest. When she does become dishonest, she might argue there is no appropriation. *Atakpu* [1994] does not assist (C is not in a process of stealing), but the second part of s 3(1) states she appropriates a second time when she decides to keep the toothbrush.

The third part is about s 2 and the *Ghosh* [1982] test. First you might argue that s 2(1)(b) applies, so that A has a belief in consent. You should point out, however, that a willingness to pay does not negate dishonesty (s 2(2)). If it falls to the *Ghosh* [1982] test, be careful to state it precisely and apply it according to your common sense.

Chapter 12

Problem answer

The first paragraph is broadly based on *Ghosh* [1982] and *Firth* (1990), and S's actions amount to fraud (s 1 Fraud Act 2006) by false representation (implied by her silence (s 2) or failing to disclose (s 3). Her actions are *Ghosh* [1982] dishonest, and she has failed to disclose when under a legal duty to do so, intending to make a gain for herself (and/or a loss to another). It is also arguable that this is a s 4 abuse of

position fraud (professional duty to protect financial position of the hospital). You could add a criticism to the effect that the new Act is very broad and the three subsections overlap. As to the purchase of supplies with orders placed online, the examiner is asking you to observe that the old deception offences could not be committed on a machine as opposed to a human mind. You should refer to s 2(5).

Chapter 13

Problem answer

As we pointed out at the start of the chapter, the topics covered in this chapter often arise with other offences or defences. In this question, on the other hand, issues surrounding accomplices arise (you should refer to chapter 10). M Molan and G Douglas, *Questions & Answers Criminal Law 2008–2009*, OUP, 6th edn, 2008 contains a raft of other examples.

Lenny

You should explain the offence of burglary. There appears to be an offence under s 9(1)(a) Theft Act 1968, but as in *Robinson* [1977], s 2 might protect him as he honestly believes he has a right in law to the property. The trespassing cases should be reviewed and you might consider whether there is an offence under s 9(1)(b) where L has entered as a trespasser and then steals (subject to what we said about dishonesty) or attempts to steal.

Morris

M has aided and abetted the burglary. Even if L is not convicted because he lacks *mens rea*, M can be as the *actus reus* is complete (refer to the derivative liability cases such as *Thornton v Mitchell* [1940] and *Howe* [1987] in chapter 10, p 126).

Chapter 14

Problem answer

1. You are told Gail suffered hypoglycaemia; do not waste time, words, and effort discussing intoxication (note the mention of alcohol in the second paragraph might lead you to consider the defence of intoxication, but in fact it is a red herring because she was not still intoxicated by

Outline answers
✶✶✶✶✶✶✶✶✶✶✶✶

alcohol when she was in the supermarket) or insanity (yet). You should mention that insulin is an external cause, and cite *Quick* [1973]. This will lead you into an explanation of (non-insane) automatism, which you should define and apply. Remember to include an analysis of the difference between specific and basic intent *and* apply to the question (note s 18 OAPA is specific intent but the criminal damage is charged as the reckless version; in light of *Caldwell* [1982] and *Heard* [2008], what is the significance of this?) noting Gail may be *Bailey* [1983] reckless in taking insulin and not eating.

2. You should indicate this is an alternative answer. You now need to explain the defence of insanity using the *M'Naghten Rules* (1843). You have to show that an internal impairment (*Sullivan* [1984]) causing the defect of reason is not enough for D to prove the defence—she must also show she did not know either the nature and quality of her act or that it was wrong. You must explain and allocate the burden of proof correctly.

Chapter 15

Problem answer

1. The rubric is quite clear—you are to tackle the *defence* only. This is duress of circumstances (there is no 'do this or else'). Explain the defence by reference to *Howe* [1987],

Hasan [2005], and in respect of circumstances, to *Conway* [1989] and *Martin* (1989).

State and apply the test from *Howe* [1987]:

- Did D feel compelled (and if he made a mistake was it a reasonable one?)
- to act as he did to avoid death/serious harm (*Baker and Wilkins* [1997], *Valderrama-Vega* [1985]) (he honestly and reasonably believed his presence was needed to consent to a procedure)
- to a person for whom he is responsible (*Wright* [2000], *Conway* [1989]) (his son), and
- would a sober person of reasonable firmness sharing D's characteristics have done the same (there are no particular *Bowen* [1996] characteristics, but you do need to reach a conclusion on whether the 'reasonable person' would have responded in the same way as D), and
- was the situation one of immediacy (*Abdul-Hussain* [1999], but a harsher line drawn in *Hasan* [2005]), and
- did D miss an opportunity to escape (*Hudson and Taylor* [1971] overruled in *Hasan* [2005]) (Harley should have taken other evasive action and not resort to a crime)?

2. In the alternative, duress is not available to murder under current law, but you might want to include analysis of whether necessity is an offshoot per *Re A* [2001] to this defence and whether it is therefore available to murder.

Glossary

Accessories Those who aid, abet, counsel, or procure the commission of the principal offence. See chapter 10.

Actual bodily harm (ABH) An element of the *actus reus* of s 47 OAPA. See chapter 5.

Actus reus The term used to classify those elements of the offence which do not relate to D's state of mind (*mens rea*). See chapter 2.

Aid, abet, counsel, or procure See **accessories**.

Assault Also known as a common assault, a technical assault, and a psychic assault; it is where D intentionally or recklessly causes V to apprehend the application of immediate unlawful force. See chapter 5.

Attempt An inchoate offence governed by the Criminal Attempts Act 1981. See chapter 9.

Automatism A defence (although the prosecution bears the burden of proof in relation to it) which negates *actus reus*. See chapters 2 and 14.

Basic intent This term relates to the type of *mens rea* in the crime charged. See **specific intent** and chapter 14.

Battery Also known as a common assault or a physical assault, it is where D intentionally or recklessly applies unlawful force to V.

Burden of proof This is the duty of a party to satisfy the fact-finder, to a standard set by law, of the facts in issue.

Causation This is a key element of result crimes, and requires the prosecution to prove D caused the result.

Chain of causation This can be established in both fact and law, but D caused the result only if there is no break in the chain. See chapter 2.

Charge This is the formal accusation that D has committed a crime. It is usually made by the police. It is not a finding of liability.

Conspiracy An inchoate offence either at common law or contrary to the Criminal Law Act 1977. See chapter 9.

Criminal law Despite the efforts of leading scholars over the centuries to provide a universally accepted definition of criminal law, one still escapes us. All leading criminal law textbooks explain why.

Definitional elements These are the components or ingredients of offences. Different crimes have different definitional elements. For ease of management, we tend to break them into the *actus reus* and *mens rea*.

Diminished responsibility A partial defence to murder, governed by s 2 Homicide Act 1957. Recently amended by the Coroners and Justice Act 2009. See chapter 7.

Elements of the offence See **definitional elements**.

Evidential burden The onus on a party to adduce sufficient evidence to make an issue 'live'.

Grievous bodily harm (GBH) An element of the *actus reus* of both ss 18 and 20 Offences Against the Person Act 1861. See chapter 5.

Homicide The act of one human being killing another human being.

Implied malice The less serious form of *mens rea* for murder. See chapter 7.

Incitement The common law offence of incitement has been replaced with offences under the Serious Crime Act 2007. See chapter 9.

Insane/insanity The defence governed by the *M'Naghten Rules*. See chapter 14.

Intoxication When we use this word, we are restricting our discussion to alcohol and other recreational drugs, eg LSD, acid. See **involuntary intoxication** and **voluntary intoxication,** and chapter 14.

Involuntary intoxication D is involuntarily intoxicated when he is not aware he is taking alcohol or a dangerous drug.

Involuntary manslaughter This is an unlawful homicide without the *mens rea* for murder. See chapter 8.

Joint venture Also known as a joint unlawful enterprise, this is where two or more defendants carry out the crime together. Each D is

Glossary

✳✳✳✳✳✳✳✳✳✳

liable for the offence. The law gets complex when one D departs from the agreed plan. See chapter 10.

Loss of self-control A partial defence to murder governed by ss 54 and 55 Coroners and Justice Act 2009. See chapter 7.

Manslaughter See **voluntary** and **involuntary manslaughter**.

Mens rea The term used to classify those elements of the offence which relate to D's state of mind. See chapter 3.

Mistake Although we refer to the 'defence' of mistake, it is an assertion by D that he did not form *mens rea*. See chapters 4 and 14.

Murder Widely regarded as the most serious crime in England, it is where D kills a human being with intention to kill or cause really serious harm. See chapter 7.

Objective In respect of *mens rea*, this describes the way in which the fact-finder assesses D's fault, and it involves assessing what the reasonable person would have thought and contrasting it to what D thought (or should have thought).

Provocation This was a partial defence to murder, governed by common law and s 3 Homicide Act 1957. It has been abolished and replaced with a new partial defence (loss of self-control). See chapter 7.

Regulatory crimes For the purposes of strict liability, regulatory crimes, also called *mala prohibita*, carry a lighter sentence and no social stigma. It is one of the factors to be considered by a judge when deciding whether a statutory provision which is silent as to *mens rea* is one of strict liability. See chapter 4.

Sentence This is the punishment imposed by a court following a plea or a verdict of guilty. This book does not deal with sentences in the criminal law.

Specific intent This term relates to the type of *mens rea* in the crime charged. See **basic intent** and chapter 14.

Subjective In respect of *mens rea*, this describes the way in which the fact-finder

assesses D's fault, and it involves assessing what D was thinking. Compare with **objective**.

Suicide pact A partial defence to murder, governed by s 4 Homicide Act 1957.

Transferred malice The doctrine where D's intention to one victim can be transferred to the actual (unintended) victim. See chapter 3.

True crime, or truly criminal For the purposes of strict liability, true crimes, also called *mala in se*, carry a heavier sentence and a social stigma. It is one of the factors to be considered by a judge when deciding whether a statutory provision which is silent as to *mens rea* is one of strict liability. See chapter 4.

Victim If there is no doubt that the complaining witness has been subject to criminal conduct, it is acceptable to refer to them as the victim (V), but if the criminal nature of the conduct is yet to be established (and in sexual offences and domestic violence that is often the case) the use of the word victim at trial would be prejudicial as it presupposes guilt. In essence, before a guilty plea or verdict, we should call the complaining witness the complainant and not use the term victim until guilt is established. However, for the sake of consistency and simplicity, we refer to all complaining witnesses as V, irrespective of charge and of whether D is acquitted or convicted, or his conviction is quashed or upheld on appeal.

Voluntary (in relation to *actus reus*) See **automatism**.

Voluntary intoxication D is voluntarily intoxicated when he is aware he is taking alcohol or a dangerous drug, even if he is not aware of its strengths or effect. See chapter 14.

Voluntary manslaughter This is where D is charged with murder and he is convicted of manslaughter because of one of the three partial defences explained in chapter 7. See also **diminished responsibility**, **provocation**, **loss of self-control**, and **suicide pact**.

Wound An element of the *actus reus* of both ss 18 and 20 Offences Against the Person Act 1861. See chapter 5.

Index

Index

✳✳✳✳✳✳✳✳✳✳✳

Index

****

Index